Great Racing Partnerships

GREAT RACING
PARTNERSHIPS

●

MICHAEL TANNER
Foreword by
PETER O'SULLEVAN

° THE °
SPORTSMAN'S
PRESS
LONDON

Published by The Sportsman's Press, 1987

British Library Cataloguing in Publication Data

Tanner, Michael
 Great racing partnerships.
 1. Jockeys—Biography.
 I. Title
 798.4'3'0922   SF336.A2
ISBN 0-948253-16-9

Printed in Great Britain at The Bath Press, Avon

Contents

List of Illustrations

Foreword by Peter O'Sullevan, O.B.E.

The relationship between horse and human is the heartbeat of racing. It is surely closest within the stable. But there is perennial evidence of subtle *rapport* between horse and jockey and all who respond to the athletic grace of the thoroughbred will delight in Michael Tanner's diligently researched and keenly observed examples of golden liaison between horse and man; from the amazing Crucifix and John Bahram Day in 1840 to another equine heroine Oh So Sharp and her star of a partner Steve Cauthen nearly 150 years later.

Just as the redoubtable Brigadier Gerard looked after his regular rider Joe Mercer – taking an uncharacteristically gentle hold going to post when the latter was recovering from serious injury, so did Steve Donoghue's favourite Diadem "help me in every way" when the great jockey rode her to one of their famous victories under the handicap of a broken wrist.

Steve seldom used the whip – never aboard Diadem – considering it invariably counter-productive; a theme which runs through this engaging book and is vehemently echoed by that kindly and masterly 19th-century cavalier George Fordham.

May it be taken to heart. And may *Great Racing Partnerships* prove the first leg of a Michael Tanner double to be completed by a similar tandem between horse and lad/lass.

ONE

Crucifix and John Bahram Day

Arguments will rage till Domesday regarding the best filly to have graced the English turf. Was "peerless" Pretty Polly superior to the mighty Sceptre, heroine of 4 classic victories, among the 20th century's female champions? Where would the relatively unheralded Virago, winner of the 1854 1,000 Guineas, fit into the pantheon of 19th-century cracks? The list of names is sufficiently lengthy to fuel many a heated discussion.

Virago was trained by John Bahram Day at Danebury, yet whether this consummate performer, who completed the City & Suburban/Great Metropolitan double on the same afternoon prior to her Guineas victory, was the best Day handled, let alone the best ever, is questionable. For Day also trained Crucifix and her claims to the aforementioned title are exceedingly strong. She was unbeaten in a dozen races (a career record for an English filly), which included 3 classics in 1840. In all 12 contests she started an odds-on favourite and according to some scribes, "Her races were won so easily that description is unnecessary."

What makes the story of Crucifix all the more fascinating is that she was partnered to most of her successes by her trainer, one of just 8 trainers to have ridden their own horse to classic victory. In point of fact Day did so on 5 occasions because in addition to the 2,000 Guineas, 1,000 Guineas and Oaks secured by Crucifix he won the 1837 1,000 Guineas on Chapeau d'Espagne and the 1838 2,000 Guineas on Grey Momus.

However the story of Crucifix and John Bahram Day transcends that of a successful partnership. In truth it is the tale of a successful triumvirate. The third figure in the alliance was one of the Turf's outstanding personalities, Lord George Bentinck, once described by Disraeli as the "Lord Paramount of the British Turf".

The third son of the 4th Duke of Portland, Bentinck decided at the age of 25 to devote the greater part of his energy to affairs of the Turf. He was an unlovable man whom his fellow Jockey Club members found arrogant, suspicious and ruthless but these qualities were particularly valuable in a racing scene riddled with skulduggery and scandal. As Member of Parliament for Kings Lynn, Bentinck fought to reform the gaming laws and for a brief period, as leader of the Protectionist party, he was talked of as a potential Prime Minister. Nevertheless it was racing that benefited most from Bentinck's talents. He developed Goodwood and replanned the Derby course; declared war on crooks, exposing the deception of Running Rein's Derby in 1844; pioneered the use of the horsebox for travelling to distant meetings when Elis won the 1836 St Leger; initiated number cloths, number boards, saddling areas and parades; banned the custom of winning owners giving presents to judges; ordered the improved supervision of weighing-out and weighing-in and revised the system of starting races which had always given plentiful opportunities for abuse. According to *Bell's Life*:

> "Honest men have to thank Lord George Bentinck for this valuable reform of the Turf, for if that nobleman had not persevered to the utmost even his powerful influence would have been blighted and a host of rotten sheep left to infect the constitution of the remaining flock."

Paradoxically for a man determined to eradicate dishonesty on the Turf, Bentinck himself was no stranger to deceit and falsehood. "He cannot but know that if the circumstances relating to Crucifix, by which he won so much money, were revealed," declared his cousin and onetime racing partner Charles Greville, "they would be considered disgraceful and dishonest."

Once the scale of Bentinck's ownership outgrew his initial establishment at Goodwood the choice of John Bahram Day as his trainer adds some credence to Greville's claims. Brilliant trainer and competent jockey though he was, Day's nickname of "Honest John" was inappropriate for a man who bet heavily and was a dab-hand at deceiving owners, bookmakers and public alike. However, like Bentinck, many of his actions typified the diversity of the Victorian character. He was a regular churchgoer and abhorred swearing and smoking.

Although Bentinck spent a fortune improving the yard and gallops at Danebury, his suspicious nature ensured an inevitable breakdown in his relationship with the equally devious Day. When the split came Bentinck sent his horses to John Kent, as honest as Day was crooked, but in 1846 he sold his entire stock on the spur of the moment for £10,000 to the Hon Edward Mostyn. Among the 218 animals was Surplice, a son of Crucifix, who achieved what had been Bentinck's lifelong ambition by winning the Derby of 1848. A few months afterwards he was dead of a heart attack while on a country walk, aged 46.

Day had already presented Bentinck with classic success via Chapeau

Crucifix: John Day junior in the saddle with John Bahram Day standing on the left

d'Espagne and Grey Momus (Firebrand, trained by Kent, won the 1842 1,000 Guineas for him) before Crucifix entered the arena. Bentinck had purchased her as a foal, along with her dam Octaviana, for 54 guineas at the dispersal sale of the virtually bankrupt Lord Chesterfield in July 1837. Tattersall's sale took place at Hyde Park Corner and mother and daughter had been walked to London from Chesterfield's Bretby Park, a journey taking two weeks to complete. No wonder Crucifix was described as the "scraggiest and most unpromising foal ever seen". She was the 22-year-old Octaviana's 15th foal, none of the previous 14 having achieved anything of note. Crucifix's sire Priam had won the 1830 Derby, ridden by John Bahram's brother Samuel, and was then exported to America. Priam was acknowledged as a perfect blood-horse in appearance, a description which could not be applied to his bay daughter. The noted equine artist Herring gives a detailed description which scarcely flatters Crucifix:

"Her head is lean, good eyes, long ears, open nostrils, neck long and light, shoulders oblique and thin and remarkably deep in brisket. Chest very narrow, arms and legs inclined to be small, her toes turn out. She is flat-sided and short in back ribs. Hips wide, quarters drooping, her thighs flat. She looks all wire and stands 16 hands."

Day's son William was more succinct but no kinder. "Crucifix had the longest neck I think I ever saw and altogether appeared the weakest mare in the world." However, handsome is as handsome does and Crucifix would soon belie her looks and even her name if Lady Grosvenor was to be believed. "You have an admirable mare," she told Bentinck, "but I don't like her name." To which the owner replied; "When she is beat, Lady Grosvenor, I will change it!"

It did not take Crucifix long to impress Day on his notoriously stiff gallops up Danebury Hill. After riding for George IV and the Duke of Grafton (for whom he won four classics) Day established himself at Danebury, four miles north-west of Stockbridge in Hampshire, in 1835. Dynastic would not be a misleading term to describe the organization at Danebury. Over 100 people were employed there under the watchful eyes of Day and his sons John junior, Samuel and William. His training methods were undeniably harsh yet, provided his horses stood this preparation, they went to post superbly fit and reaped the rewards accordingly.

Nevertheless a regime such as this meant Day's horses trod a thin line between soundness and infirmity, none more so than Crucifix. The narrowness of her chest left her prey to "speedy-cut" and although her sire was a model of docility, Crucifix inherited the unstable and impetuous temperament of her dam. These traits soon manifested themselves when Day "tried" Crucifix as a yearling with the two-year-old Seth at a difference of 2 stone. Seth had wins at Epsom and Newmarket to his credit but, ridden by John Bahram, he had no answer to Crucifix (William Day up) until some errant bystanders began to wander across the gallop. The filly immediately took fright and ran-out. However the message had been crystal clear and as soon as Bentinck was familiarized with the news he entered her in every race worth winning.

Crucifix made her debut in the July Stakes. Danebury knew her to be a good thing, information that could not be concealed for ever and she was being heavily backed days before the race. Bentinck was enraged at the market being stolen from under his nose and ordered Day to contact the other trainers and offer to scratch Crucifix if they would guarantee him half the prize money in return. Lord George failed to get his way and at the last minute Crucifix was allowed to run. Ridden by John Day junior she beat Currency hard-held by two lengths at odds of 6/5 on. Two days later John Bahram took the mount in the Chesterfield Stakes. Cogniscent of the filly's impetuosity, the other jockeys tried to bring about her downfall by ruining the start and almost succeeded. Crucifix lost 50 yards and was beaten $\frac{1}{2}$ length by Iris, winner of the Woodcote at Epsom, to whom she conceded 9lb on the strength of her July Stakes' victory. However a false start was declared and the runners recalled, Crucifix taking the rerun in a canter by 2 lengths. "Crucifix is one of the finest mares ever seen," opined one contemporary observer who, with one eye already on the classics, concluded: "We look upon her performance this day as showing every quality essential to the Epsom course." Indeed, Bentinck was already making hefty wagers to that effect.

Crucifix won twice at Goodwood (the Lavant and Molecomb, both at 4/1 on) and was then rested till the autumn when she won 5 races at Newmarket. John Day junior partnered her in the Hopeful Stakes on October 1st (5/2 on) and to a walkover in a Sweepstakes the following afternoon. By contrast, the Clearwell Stakes run on October 15th was not such a cakewalk. In wet, gloomy conditions the field were delayed 10 minutes at the start and despite the presence of her stablemate Capote, put in the race to act as a calming influence in just these circumstances, Crucifix (5/1 on) began to grow anxious and in the race itself only defeated General Yates's colt Gibraltar (received 7lb) by a length. Her task in the Prendergast Stakes three days later proved far easier since only Colonel Anson's Nicholas opposed her besides the trusty Capote and, carrying her trainer on this occasion, she won as she pleased.

The Danebury alliance decided to execute one more gamble and declared Crucifix for the Criterion Stakes at the end of the month. The weather turned out even colder and windier than on her last visit and Crucifix was in a foul mood before the race. Victories in the July, Clearwell and Prendergast Stakes earned her a 9lb penalty and it was all she could manage to force a dead-heat with Gibraltar. In her defence there was a suspicion that she had sprained a suspensory and a run-off was declined, the stakes being divided. Day's training methods were beginning to take their toll.

With huge bets riding on the outcome of the Oaks, Bentinck could not risk having Crucifix fired since the lengthy period of recuperation would eliminate Epsom. Consequently she was blistered, causing her classic preparation to be unorthodox to say the least, and her very participation touch and go. "She is not able to gallop," reported The Sportsman's correspondent in February, "though she is taken out and hobbled into an apology for a canter." Day somehow got two sweats out of her before the 2,000 Guineas on May 5th, in which she started 11/8 on to beat five opponents for the £1,450 prize.

Needless to say there was one false start and Crucifix was last away but

Crucifix winning the Oaks

as the Angelica colt set the early pace John Bahram confidently made up his ground to take the lead at the Bushes and win in a canter from Confederate. Two days afterwards the partnership beat the Danebury second string Rose Bianca just as comfortably in the 1,000 Guineas at odds of 10/1 on.

Notwithstanding these facile triumphs time was fast running out for Crucifix and her associates. The ground in the early summer of 1840 was akin to iron and the filly's legs were constantly exhibiting tell-tale signs of wear and tear, and a week before Epsom it was feared they had gone completely. Oaks day dawned propitiously. "There was no dust, little wind and sufficient sun to warm without baking the visitor," said *The Times* before stating: "It was well known to everybody at all acquainted with the betting that Crucifix would win." Bentinck himself stood to win £40,000.

The race was due off at 2p.m. but the 15 runners were an hour at the post. It took the starter 16 attempts to get them away and when he did Crucifix was left fully 50 yards. Bentinck was blithely unconcerned. "She could not lose but on the contrary could afford to flirt with the best of them for half a day." Lalla Rookh led them up the hill followed by Welfare and Teleta with Crucifix and Day bringing up the rear some three lengths adrift of the penultimate horse. However the pace was so pedestrian that they had burst to the front before the top of the hill was reached and were two lengths clear entering the straight. Toward the finish the second and third began to make a fight of it and Crucifix won by a dwindling $\frac{1}{2}$ length. "Rather cleverly but not in the style of her other triumphs," said *The Times*. Of course, no one outside Danebury knew the exact state of her legs and that the Oaks would almost certainly finish her for good. This did not stop her unscrupulous owner laying against her for the St Leger (she was now a 9/2 second favourite behind the Derby second Launcelot at 4s) even though he knew the chances of her getting to Doncaster were remote.

During that shambolic hour down at the Epsom start Crucifix had struck into herself and before her next intended outing in Goodwood's Drawing Room Stakes her near-fore filled alarmingly. Day blistered Crucifix once again but she had run her last race, though Bentinck declined to inform the public of this fact until 4 days before the Leger. On a line through Gibraltar, beaten 2 necks by Launcelot, a fit Crucifix would have won a fourth classic.

Crucifix's son Surplice (by Touchstone) achieved for Edward Mostyn the Derby victory which eluded Bentinck and through her daughter Rosemary she is the ancestress of Double Life, foundation mare of the Someries Stud, the third dam of Meld who produced the 1966 Derby winner Charlottown.

Crucifix died at Danebury in November 1858, wasted and listless, her withers "as sharp as a knife", having been barren for 6 years. She was buried beside the stallion Bay Middleton under a cedar tree planted in memoriam by the Days. Within 2 years John Bahram Day was also dead, spending the last 5 years of his life in retirement after one patron too many (the notorious moneylender Henry Padwick) lost a bet thanks to a piece of typical Day chicanery and dismissed him.

The image bequeathed to posterity by John Bahram Day is, at best, enigmatic, at worst somewhat blemished. He both rode and trained classic winners yet was not averse to soiling his hands.

Not so his immortal partner Crucifix, whose praises were sung in Thormanby's *Kings of the Turf*, wherein it was written of her Oaks performance:

> "She could have given any of them four times that distance up that hill, round that turn and down the straight and then have won hands down. In fact it would have been impossible to handicap Crucifix that day with any mare of her age, so supreme was her superiority over all her contemporaries."

Crucifix

CRUCIFIX

Bay filly 1837
Ran 12   Won 12   Value of Races Won £10,287

Crucifix			
	Priam	Emilius	Orville / Emily
		Cressida	Whiskey / Young Giantess
	Octaviana	Octavian	Stripling / Daughter of Oberon
		Daughter of Shuttle	Shuttle / Zara

TWO

Lady Elizabeth and George Fordham

Thirty years after Lady Elizabeth retired some judges still considered her the most brilliant two-year-old to set foot on the Turf. Writing in 1901 Sydenham Dixon, for so long "Vigilant" of *The Sportsman*, dared suggest she was "absolutely the best two-year-old that ever lived", though he quickly added the disclaimer that memories of Crucifix, Wheel of Fortune, St Simon and Ormonde "make one a little dubious about penning such a sweeping assertion".

However, racing would be a pretty dull affair without opinion, as is reinforced by the age-old debate concerning the best jockey of all time. Whatever conclusions reached by present day historians, the jockeys of the Victorian era were unanimous in their verdict – George Fordham was the best. John Osborne claimed that Fordham was in a class above all others, Archer included. Invariably he outwitted Archer, who could never quite fathom his tactics, as he revealed at Newmarket one day:

> "Fordham was cluck-clucking at his mount for the whole of the race. I thought I had him beaten 2 or 3 times in the 2 miles. But with his infernal cluck-clucking he was always coming again. Still 200 yards from home I supposed I had him dead settled. I'll cluck-cluck you, I thought – and at that moment he swoops down on me and beats me easily.'"

Fordham took great delight in "kidding" whether he was riding against his arch rival or young greenhorns. A few hundred yards from the post he would feign distress and then just as the youngster sensed victory Fordham would sail past to the amusement and financial gain of his countless supporters who understandably nicknamed him "The Demon". If Fordham was a demon in a finish he could boast neither Archer's clinical efficiency at the start nor his nerve during a race. As a four-stone apprentice of 14 a bad fall damaged his knee and, more significantly some suggested, impaired his nerve from then on. Certainly he could not match Archer's success in the hurly-burly of the Derby (he only won once from 20 rides) but whether this was due to a lack of courage descending Tattenham Hill as his critics maintained is doubtful. After all Fordham won 5 races for the Oaks over the same course.

Henry Custance, himself the winner of 5 classics, also sided with the Fordham lobby in his book of racing recollections.

"In speaking of one whom I consider all round to be the finest jockey I ever saw or rode against, it is needless for me to say that I refer to my dear old friend George Fordham. It is quite impossible for me to mention all the fine races I have seen him ride."

Even John Porter and Mat Dawson, for whom Fred Archer rode innumerable winners, went on record as believing Fordham to be the superior all-round jockey. The statistics speak for themselves – 2,369 winners including 16 classics, 14 times champion jockey (once jointly).

As a man Fordham had many appealing characteristics, not least of which was his kindhearted nature. On one occasion after he had lost a small race by a head to a horse owned by the widow of his first guv'ner Dick Drewitt he said to Sir John Astley, "Well, you know, Sir John, Mrs Drewitt has not been able to pay her rent and all through the race I could not help thinking of that damned rent, and you know I ought just to have won." Fordham's one failing was drink which, along with ill-health, enforced a period of retirement between 1876 and 1878. Before the 1872 City & Suburban, Henry Woolcott, the trainer of Fordham's mount Digby Grand, entered the paddock carrying a bottle of port with which he intended to stimulate the animal's racing instincts. Fordham insisted he test the vintage first, and instantly consumed the whole bottle! He then mounted Digby Grand and won the race.

Fordham's charity extended to his behaviour in the saddle for he frequently rode without whip or spur. To an apprentice mounting prior to the Cesarewitch he said, "Dear me, what a pretty whip that is, my boy, but what a pity it is that these pretty things lose so many races. Don't you think that you had better leave it behind?" – whereupon he placed it in his pocket and walked away.

Fordham's reluctance to strike a horse (except in the last few strides), his judgement of pace and lightness of touch combined to make him the ideal partner for a two-year-old. Moreover, his ungainly style – he rode with very short leathers and slewed his body round until it was almost sideways – proved so deceptive that few could tell if a short head victory was gained with the proverbial "ton" in hand or by mere "kidding". The

George Fordham

result was that he was able to give two-year-olds the tenderest possible race. He once told Mr Leopold Rothschild:

> "When I get down to the post on these two-year-olds, and I feel their little hearts beating under my legs I think, why not let them have an easy race, win if they can but don't frighten them."

In the summer of 1867 Fordham was able to exercise his genius with two-year-olds on Lady Elizabeth. She was a bay by Trumpeter (third in the 1859 Derby) out of Miss Bowzer and stood a trifle under 16 hands. Her head and neck were perfection and she possessed magnificent shoulders, great depth and big wide hips. Only her straight thighs and hocks offended the eye although her high-mettled, fiery demeanour constituted more than enough shortcomings on the score of temperament. The "marriage" between the flighty but beautiful Lady Elizabeth and the sympathetic George Fordham seemed one made in heaven. However, the purity of this partnership was obliged to withstand the shadiest possible influences because Lady Elizabeth was trained by the artful John Day junior for Henry, 4th Marquis of Hastings whose reckless penchant for gambling had also seen him fall under the spell of the infamous moneylender Henry Padwick.

John Day assumed control of Danebury in 1845 and was already an experienced trainer when he was introduced to the young Oxford undergraduate Harry Hastings. The latter's love of gambling and thirst for popular acclaim inevitably decreed a career on the Turf and what better associates than the Days of Danebury who, in company with the ex-jailbird and pugilist turned MP, John Gully, among others, had formed the renowned, "Danebury Confederacy" that extracted a fortune from the bookmakers in the 1840s. By 1862 Gully was a dying man and Danebury could well accommodate a fearless replacement. Hastings suited the role to a tee.

In July 1862 Hastings, on Day's advice, bought a filly called Consternation for 95 guineas. Running in the name of "Mr Weysford", she won twice for him at Dover and Warwick, on the latter occasion with Fordham in the saddle. Hastings made plans for expansion because 1863 marked his coming-of-age and an unlimited supply of funds. Abandoning his *nom de course*, the Hastings colours of "scarlet and white hoop, white cap" immediately became a familiar sight throughout the land. The Days had never been trainers to spare their charges, at home or on the track, and for the Marquis to punt his horses had to run. His first runner was a two-year-old colt called Garotter at Northampton in March and before the season's end he had run a further 17 times, winning 3 races. Another juvenile, Tippler, ran 10 times, twice over a mile on one afternoon at Brighton. A third, Recap, was twice subjected to 2 races on the same day.

The pattern of Hastings' brief sojourn on the Turf was set. He raced his horses hard and he attacked the Ring vigorously, sometimes recklessly. However, by the advent of Lady Elizabeth in 1867 his health and fortunes, ravaged by a dissolute lifestyle that made him appear far older than his 25 years, had begun to nosedive. His bitter rival Henry Chaplin, from whom he had stolen the hand of Lady Florence Paget – the "Pocket Venus" – won the Derby with Hermit causing Hastings to sustain debts of £120,000. His saving grace throughout a trying year was the phenomenal Lady Elizabeth whose 12 victories recouped most of these losses.

The Danebury juveniles of 1867 were an exceptional crop, for besides Lady Elizabeth they included at least 5 other crackerjacks. Athena won 10 of her 14 races and would eventually be placed in both the 1,000 Guineas and Oaks; Europa won 6 from 7 in a short career extending from Ascot to Goodwood; See-Saw won 5 times and later won the Royal Hunt Cup and the Cambridgeshire; Mameluke won Stockbridge's valuable Donnington Post Stakes; lastly, a backward colt called The Earl won 4 times but was fated to play a more sinister role in Hastings' downfall the following season. But even in that strong field Lady Elizabeth was the undisputed queen of them all.

She had run, and won, 4 races before Hastings' disastrous plunge on the Derby, commencing in typical Danebury fashion, with two wins in two days at Northampton in early April. Her debut was made in the modest Sulby Stakes over 4 furlongs, worth a paltry £55, in which Fordham brought her home 5 lengths to the good. After the second victory, in the Althorp Park Stakes (a much more lucrative event of £530), the Salisbury Stakes on May 9th proved a sterner test as she only prevailed by a neck from Lord Palmerston. The Weston Stakes at Bath, a week afterwards, would go some way toward establishing her true ability since, in the words of *Bell's Life*, the field included "some good-looking, clever-shaped animals" such as John Porter's Blue Gown (2/1 favourite) recently victorious at the subsequently discontinued Ascot spring meeting, Formosa (who would ultimately win 4 classics) and Mr Pryor's game little colt Grimston. In addition, Lady Elizabeth (5/1) had to concede the Porter colt 2lb.

A bitterly cold east wind blew across the downs contributing to a less than satisfactory start. Blue Gown got away particularly badly and Fordham, just ahead of him, saw to it that he remained trapped on the rails. Grimston, meanwhile, had set sail for the winning post and looked to have the race in safe keeping until Fordham, realizing the seriousness of the situation, got to work on the filly and snatched the spoils by a short head. The unfortunate Blue Gown had twice been thwarted when trying to get through into a challenging position. He would exact his revenge at a later date.

Grimston faced Lady Elizabeth again at Epsom, the day after Hermit's Derby. He had already won at the meeting and at the weights held a splendid chance of reversing the Bath result. There were several false starts, after one of which Bessy Dixon completed the entire course. Lady Elizabeth became very fractious at these delays and once the field was successfully dispatched Fordham allowed her to stride along in front rather than restrain her any longer. However on meeting the rising ground near the finish Grimston staged a tremendous last-ditch rally to force a dead-heat. The filly looked desperately worn out but Fordham was a master in match races and in the run-off she led all the way to win a magnificent duel by a head. Lady Elizabeth had indeed salvaged some of Hastings' money yet even as she was returning to Danebury he lost it again when Achievement was beaten in the Oaks.

Although the Marquis settled this debt before Ascot commenced a fortnight later, another calamitous week here could have destroyed him once and for all. Competitive races ensured the gambler a decent betting market. Hastings had to know if Lady Elizabeth could be counted upon to play her part in the New Stakes. To this end a secret trial was arranged at Danebury for the Tuesday of Ascot week. To maintain the subterfuge Day

Going down for the New Stakes, 1867

departed for Ascot as usual and left the arrangements to his head man Joseph Enoch. The trial took place over 6 furlongs on the adjacent Stock-bridge racecourse at the ungodly hour of 3 o'clock in the morning. Lady Elizabeth received just 2lb from the three-year-old Challenge and 10lb from the five-year-old Lord Ronald, that is 27 and 32lb less than weight for age. A second five-year-old, Pantaloon, was put in with a very light weight to make the running but the gallop was such that he could never get to the front. Lady Elizabeth waited on her elders and then cruised past to win by a couple of lengths without breaking sweat. The magnitude of this perfor-mance was not lost on Danebury. Lord Ronald had just won the Salisbury Cup under top weight and elsewhere had successfully conceded 66lb to some two-year-olds with winning form (later on Challenge would win 5 races off the reel including the Liverpool Summer Cup). Hastings lost no time in placing a huge bet of £16,000 on the filly. His luck was about to change with a vengeance.

The New Stakes followed immediately on the Gold Cup in which Fordham rode one of his most powerful finishes to land the prize on Hastings' Lecturer. As a result these winnings went straight on to Lady Elizabeth, one of the heaviest investments even Hastings had made.

Starting at evens in a field of 12 the filly broke smartly and won in a canter by 6 lengths "like another Blink Bonny" according to *Bell's Life*. *The Times* was equally enthusiastic.

> "Lady Elizabeth, with her 5lb penalty, made such an exhibition of her field, including one or two candidates for Derby honours next year, that the backers of Rabican (beaten into fourth), who has already found his way into Derby books, must have been disconcerted."

Blink Bonny's Derby success of 1857 was only the second by a filly. Hastings was confident that Fordham and his beloved Lady Elizabeth would change all that.

However, betting opportunities there would be aplenty before May 1868 and Hastings now had the bit firmly between his teeth. Lady Elizabeth won twice at Stockbridge in June, the Eltham and Troy Stakes (both £1,000-plus events), beating The Earl in the former and Rabican in the latter, and received two walkovers. Hastings could not capitalize on these successes due to ludicrous starting prices but the July Stakes threw up a serious challenger in the Duke of Hamilton's filly Leonie which promised distinct possibilities. "There is always something exciting in the contest for the stakes which take their name from the meeting," observed *The Times*. "On this occasion Leonie and Lady Elizabeth were the heroines and a fine race was anticipated between them." Leonie had defeated Athena for the Hamilton (Post) Stakes after a run-off – incidentally Fordham's only reverse in 7 races at Stockbridge that day. The Duke of Hamilton's support for Leonie enabled Hastings to obtain odds of 5/4 on Lady Elizabeth. Knowing his filly to be some 11–18lb superior to Athena he made hay. Fordham allowed Leonie to lead until the dip before unleashing Lady Elizabeth. "She never suffered Leonie to touch her," said *The Times*, "and won with 10lb in hand".

The partnership thus extended its undefeated sequence to eleven (including two walkovers) and took a well-deserved rest until the £4,410 Middle Park Plate in October. By now few people, least of all Hastings and Fordham, thought Lady Elizabeth could be beaten and Day was wont to talk of her in the same breath as Crucifix and Virago. While it was true her misbehaviour at the start often cost her several lengths she could afford to give 3 or 4 lengths away because nothing could live with her once she got into her stride. No filly ever possessed a finer constitution and she never left an oat despite the extreme demands made of her.

Fifteen opponents faced her for the second running of the Middle Park, "altogether a finer lot of two-year-olds has not been seen for some years." These included Formosa (winner of 3 races since Bath, including a victory over Leonie and Athena in the Chesterfield Stakes), Mat Dawson's leggy filly Lady Coventry and 3 from John Porter's yard, Blue Gown (a Royal Ascot winner), Rosicrucian and Green Sleeve, "a blood-like, racing-looking filly". Nevertheless Danebury saw no reason for faint-hearts. "The amount of money that went on Lady Elizabeth was large even for these gambling days," said *The Times*. "Lord Hastings put down the money as if the race was over." He had in fact backed her to win £50,000.

A day of teeming rain did nothing to cool the even-money favourite's antics at the start. Lady Elizabeth repeatedly broke away and when the flag finally fell she was almost sitting on her haunches. Fordham was unperturbed and with less than 2 furlongs to run he still had the filly's head pulled round to his knee. Lady Coventry and Green Sleeve vied for the lead and when the former weakened only Rosicrucian (Porter's favoured runner) could make any inroads on Green Sleeve's advantage. Lady Elizabeth trailed in fifth with a rueful Fordham muttering, "I ought to have won many a length."

Hastings was devastated, not so much at the blow to his pocket as that to his heart. "Still, when we consider how often Lady Elizabeth has been called upon during the season," wrote one contemporary chronicler, "her having to lower her colours cannot create much wonderment." Hastings was determined that Lady Elizabeth be given the opportunity of redeeming her reputation as quickly as possible and a £1,000-a-side match was arranged between her and the Duke of Newcastle's colt Julius to be run 2 days after the Middle Park.

Matches were an integral part of the mid-Victorian racing scene. After dinner in the Jockey Club Rooms those owners willing to make matches wrote on slips of paper the names of the horses they wished to run and handed them to Admiral Rous who would examine the slips, make the match and set the weights and distance.

Now Julius was a three-year-old who had just won the Cesarewitch carrying 8 stone, a record for that age, and had run third in the St Leger. Rous set his weight at 8st 11lb. The filly, 1 year younger, carried 8st 2lb which amounted to a stone more than the weight-for-age scale. In these circumstances Julius had to start favourite (11/10 on) and Hastings could therefore wager with abandon. Fordham, too, could be excused for believing victory essential. He had ridden a stinker in the Middle Park and also got pipped a head on The Earl in the Bedford Stakes. He owed Hastings a victory.

The match was a classic of its kind with no quarter asked or given from the outset. "They ran locked to within 3 or 4 strides of home," reported *The Times*, "whereupon Fordham 'put on the screw' and landed Lady Elizabeth the winner by the shortest of heads." To the greatest private performance ever put up by a two-year-old Lady Elizabeth could now add the finest public performance accomplished by a two-year-old. It was a proud

Hastings who greeted a relieved Fordham and an exhausted Lady Elizabeth. He could not hope to restore the week's losses but she had restored her prestige which was far more important to him. He was certain she *would* win the Derby in 1868.

Lady Elizabeth won neither Derby nor any other race in 1868. Furthermore, barely a year after his darling seemingly put him on the brink of his finest hour, Hastings was dead. Despite the herculean efforts of Lady Elizabeth, Hastings was heavily in debt by the end of the 1867 season. He had already sold his Scottish estates and now was obliged to sell his racehorses. He could not bear to part with either Lady Elizabeth or The Earl however, and they were bought-in for 6,500 and 6,100 guineas respectively. Even this sale of 21 yearlings and 24 horses in training could not save him. His immediate rescue depended upon Henry Padwick. Everyone knew his ultimate salvation lay with Lady Elizabeth.

It was not to be. Lady Elizabeth wintered badly and there is no question that the tremendous battle with Julius broke her. She grew nervous and irritable. The grand doer became a delicate feeder. She had been backed to win so much money in the Derby that Day was afraid to try her and confirm his worst fears that the strenuous two-year-old career had sapped

The Ascot Betting Ring, 1867

all her spirit. In the early spring odds of 6/1 could be had about her and these rapidly contracted to 7/4 by Derby day thanks to a stream of fictitious reports from Danebury as to her continued prowess. "I take off my hat to that darling," said Mr Punch, "and if wishes were horses and beggars could ride, I'm the beggar that would ride her into glory and win the battle of Hastings." With the benefit of hindsight, an anonymous poet in *Bell's Life* obviously knew better and spelled out the danger.

> *For Lady Elizabeth in spite of her wins*
> *Will have to cave in when the fighting begins*
> *And all you gay gallants of old London Town*
> *Must put your spare cash on old Bonny Blue Gown.*

On a warm May afternoon Day arranged for Lady Elizabeth to be saddled in Sherwood's stables near the start to avoid unnecessary strain on her temperament. The ruse failed and she was fretful and sweating profusely. The instant Fordham dropped into the saddle she attempted to buck him off. In the race itself she was never seen with a chance as Blue Gown headed King Alfred to win by ½ length. On the Friday she was beaten out of sight in the Oaks with Cannon riding and was booed by the masses who had once adored her. Fordham switched to the winner Formosa. As in the 1,000 Guineas, the placed horses were Lady Coventry and Athena causing the decline of Lady Elizabeth to be all the more easily charted. On a line through her stablemate the Lady Elizabeth of 1867 would have won both Guineas for sure and quite possibly the Oaks and Leger.

The fact that Lady Elizabeth could scarcely raise a gallop, coupled with the eleventh-hour scratching from the Derby of The Earl, who had beaten Blue Gown at Newmarket and 10 days after Epsom won the Grand Prix de Paris, really put the cat among the pigeons. Day must have known the filly had lost all semblance of form yet he allowed Padwick to persuade Hastings that withdrawing the colt from the Derby was in his best interests. When The Earl won 3 more races at Ascot within 3 days of returning from France and Lady Elizabeth finished last in the Prince of Wales's Stakes the storm finally broke. Admiral Rous was overheard to say that had he taken as much laudanum as had been given Lady Elizabeth he would have found himself in his coffin. The remark was reproduced in *The Sporting Life* and then quoted in the *Pall Mall Gazette* which resulted in the Admiral writing his infamous "Spider and the Fly" letter to *The Times* and triggering one of the Turf's most sensational *causes célèbres*. He denied the laudanum comment but otherwise attacked Danebury on all fronts. He maintained that the Days knew in March that Lady Elizabeth (after a rough spin with Athena) had lost her form and that they reversed a commission to back her for the 1,000 Guineas. Hastings was constantly denied the opportunity of watching her gallop, he added.

> "Lord Hastings has been shamefully deceived. In justice... I state that he stood to win £35,000 by The Earl and did not hedge his stake money. Then you will ask, 'Why did he scratch him?' What can the poor fly demand from the spider in whose web he is enveloped?"

Hastings strongly resented any suggestion that he had been duped and the "spider", Padwick, and Day instituted libel suits against Rous but the case never came to court. In any event the bubble had burst. Hastings owed the ring £40,000; The Earl broke down and missed the St Leger; he no longer loved his wife. On October 19th he paid his last visit to Newmarket and saw Lady Elizabeth and Fordham finish third of five in a lowly plate. Three weeks later, on November 10th, he was dead, his body wasted by drink (officially he died of Bright's Disease) and his soul destroyed by gambling. He was 26.

Lady Elizabeth passed to his widow and ran once more in May 1869 in the Earl Spencer Plate at Northampton, ridden by Cannon. She came nowhere and subsequently achieved nothing at stud.

So ended the "spider and the fly" drama and the career of a filly who was still spoken of in the time of Sceptre and Pretty Polly as the greatest two-year-old ever seen on the English Turf. Lady Elizabeth's 12 victories were worth £9,165 in stake money, a mere drop in the ocean to Hastings. To George Fordham those dozen triumphs represented an enduring link with possibly the best animal he ever rode. He died at Slough, aged 50, on October 11th, 1887. The brass plate on his coffin carried an apt commentary on not just his own career but also those of Hastings and his beloved Lady Elizabeth: "'Tis the pace that kills."

LADY ELIZABETH

Bay filly 1865
Ran 18   Won 12   Placed 1   Value of Races Won £9,165

Lady Elizabeth	Trumpeter	Orlando	Touchstone / Vulture
		Cavatina	Redshank / Oxygen
	Miss Bowzer	Hesperus	Bay Middleton / Plenary
		Mangosteen	Emilius / Mustard

THREE

Wheel of Fortune and Fred Archer

When quizzed on the exceptional horses with which he had been associated Fred Archer understandably held the likes of St Simon and Ormonde in the highest regard, yet he always ended the conversation by saying, "Don't forget the mare. She was wonderfully good." The mare in question was the diminutive Wheel of Fortune. This tiny filly, standing only 15.1 hands, and the gangling 5 feet $8\frac{1}{2}$ inch jockey seemed an unlikely combination, for in the words of the Duke of Portland, "his long legs encircled her and she looked like a large polo pony," yet together they won ten races, including the 1,000 Guineas and Oaks of 1879, before the "Wheel" broke down at York in her last race prior to the St Leger. Denied the opportunity of thrashing the classic colts, Wheel of Fortune retired to stud where she proved a comparative failure. Archer rode on for another 7 seasons to accumulate 2,748 winners (including 21 classics) and 13 jockeys' championships (8 times with a total exceeding 200) until in a fit of delirium brought on by severe wasting, depression and typhoid fever he shot himself on November 8th, 1886.

What heights Archer and Wheel of Fortune might have scaled had fate not intervened is, of course, conjectural. The filly might easily have won a third classic and progressed unbeaten through the Gold Cup and other top races the following season, thereby setting herself on a pedestal impossible to topple. Archer might have amassed a total of classics and overall winners beyond the reach of Piggott and Richards. There is, consequently, an air of tragedy surrounding the partnership between the Wheel and Fred Archer, a profound sense of sorrow, albeit mixed with joy, which the passing of a century has scarcely diminished.

The last of Archer's classic victories was gained on Ormonde whose trainer John Porter summarized the jockey's character as well as anyone.

"His whole heart and soul were in the business he had in hand. He was almost invariably the first to weigh-out, the first at the starting post, the first away

Wheel of Fortune and Fred Archer

when the flag fell, and, as the record shows, very often the first to pass the winning post. I am afraid he was not too scrupulous. Very masterful, he generally had pretty much his own way, especially in minor races. If he did not want a horse to run he never hesitated to suggest to the owner that he should keep the horse in the stable that day. In short, Fred Archer was a powerful personality as well as a brilliantly successful jockey.''

The story that a young Archer was once found in tears because he could not ride both winners in a dead-heat may be apocryphal but it serves to illustrate his attitude to his chosen profession. Naturally for one so successful Archer made a lot of money (at one time he was thought to be worth £$\frac{1}{4}$ million but his will was proved at £60,000) and his ability to look after it earned him the reputation (partly cultivated) of being a bit of a skinflint. ''That damned long-legged, tin-scraping young devil,'' is how Archer's mentor Mat Dawson was to describe him, ''tin'' being the Victorian slang for money. Nevertheless, the ''Tinman'' must not be remembered as a cold, ungenerous fish. According to his sister Alice:

''Fred had a great deal of character. He was gentle, but he took no liberties himself and no one ever thought of taking one with him. And he was always so quiet. There was never any ranting and raving. He would also rather be two minutes early than two minutes late. Fred knew we were short of money. At first he would send postal orders for a few shillings whenever he could spare them. Later it ran to fivers and, at last, to big sums. Mother and father always owed long bills and Fred always paid them."

Within this taut, self-contained, highly-introverted personality lay the seeds of not only unmitigated ambition but also the depression which eventually killed him.

Archer's unquenchable thirst for success is all the more remarkable when one considers the physical handicaps he overcame. When he joined Dawson's Heath House stable as an apprentice in 1868 he weighed barely 4st 11lb; in his first championship season of 1874 his minimum weight had risen to 6 stone and by the time he rode Wheel of Fortune he struggled to do 8st 7lb. During the winter his weight would rise to around 10 stone which ensured frequent doses of a vicious purgative known as "Archer's Mixture" and a diet consisting of castor oil, a biscuit and a small glass of champagne at midday. In October 1886 this strict regime enabled him to lose 6lb in two days on his last visit to Ireland but he failed to make the 8st 6lb weight on St Mirin in the Cambridgeshire upon his return. The pound overweight cost him the race (he was beaten a head) and by the end of a cold afternoon his undernourished constitution finally began to cave in. He contracted a fever yet continued to ride over the remaining two days of the meeting and actually rode five winners (including Ormonde) on the last day with Blanchland, fittingly for Lord Falmouth, his 2,748th and final success. He rode at Brighton and Lewes the following week – Tommy Tittlemouse on the Thursday was his last mount – before admitting defeat and returning to Newmarket. Four days later he was dead.

Archer's physical decline inevitably gnawed away at his overloaded psyche and he became increasingly neurotic as he grew older, particularly after the death at birth of his first child and then that of his 23-year-old wife Helen Rose (Dawson's niece) after the birth of his second surviving daughter Nellie in 1884. He vowed that he would slow down. "I shan't put myself out and ride quite so much. I've headed the list for eleven years but I've got so many things to look after that I can often do more useful work at home than in going about the country to ride," he told *The Illustrated Sporting and Dramatic News*. With little else to live for Archer soon broke his pledge. In 1885 he established a championship record of 246 wins from 667 mounts, a feat best appreciated by remembering that Gordon Richards' record of 259 in 1933 came from 975 rides in an age when travelling from meeting to meeting was infinitely easier and more comfortable.

If Archer's appearance and personality resembled that of an unobtrusive bank clerk (he was afraid of the dark for example), he became the devil incarnate once astride a horse. It was often said that although Archer's father William had been a good enough jockey to win a Grand National, Fred's persona in fact came from his mother Emma. "She was a big, fine-looking woman with handsome aquiline features – people always used to say she must have had some good blood in her veins," said one neighbour. "One's first impression of Archer would have been that of a gentleman by birth." Whatever the source of his genius Archer was soon riding in pony and donkey races in and around Cheltenham, his family's home town. It was through a mutual friend that Archer came to Mat Dawson, who would eventually train a total of 28 classics, half of which were partnered by Frederick James Archer.

The young apprentice got his first ride, aged 12, on the mare Honoria in the Newmarket Town Plate of 1869, where they finished last. However, after a victory on Maid of Trent in a Bangor steeplechase for Mrs Willins, an acquaintance of his father, he broke his duck on the flat at Chesterfield on September 28th 1870 when he rode Athol Daisy, trained by John Peart at Malton, to win a nursery. In all he had 15 rides that season, winning 2 and being placed second no fewer than 9 times.

The Heath House stable jockey during this formative period of Archer's career was Thomas French. A fine horseman and skilful race rider, French was unmerciful with whip and spur. Moreover he was considerably taller than most jockeys and was forced to waste hard. It is therefore not difficult to imagine why and how Archer's career took the course it did. The ultimate, tragic irony is that French also died young, from consumption brought about by wasting, at exactly the same age, 29, as Archer. The reputation for undue severity which Archer earned in his early years clung to him for the rest of his life even though he modified his style toward the end. In 1884 he told an interviewer:

> "It's a great mistake to knock a horse about, and I know that a few years back I was a severe rider but I've learnt better by experience. I rarely hit a horse more than twice in a finish now and I rarely or never have rowels to my spurs. You can hurt a horse almost as much without if you want to but it's bad policy to hurt them."

In fact Archer could ride any sort of race – he could wait or go on and was an excellent judge of pace. However, his forte was the finish where his long legs appeared to wrap themselves round his horse's flanks to virtually lift the beast past the post whilst his tactic of riding with a loose rein, so that he could sit up the horse's neck, was calculated to catch the judge's eye in any tight conclusion. Archer's steely resolve had no finer testing ground than Epsom where he proved a terror down Tattenham Hill. Although he won 5 Derbies, that total would undoubtedly have risen had he always ridden freelance rather than abided by his retainer for Lord Falmouth in whose colours he completed 7 of his 13 rides, winning only on Silvio in 1877. His performance on Bend Or one year later has quite rightly entered Turf folklore. Twenty-five days before the Derby, while riding work on Newmarket Heath, Archer was savaged by Muley Edris, a horse to whom he had administered some dire thrashings in the hope of subduing the animal's vicious temper (he had actually got Muley Edris to win races). The demented beast bit through the muscles of Archer's arm so badly that the Derby on Bend Or would have seemed out of the question to any ordinary mortal. But Archer was extraordinary. To regain his riding weight he had to shed a stone in the week prior to the race and was obliged to ride with his almost useless arm strapped to a steel brace under his silks. He came round Tattenham Corner so close to the rails that the nearer of his long legs had to be lifted onto Bend Or's withers and then set about catching the clear leader Robert the Devil. A hundred yards from the post Archer, forgetting his incapacity, went for his whip and dropped it. No matter. Somehow he communicated his fanatical commitment to Bend Or and they got up to pip Robert the Devil by a head in a breathtaking finish.

A few paragraphs can hardly do justice to a genius like Archer but they are vital if one is to appreciate what kind of man contributed the human half of the partnership under review. Horse and rider complemented each other in so many ways. The Wheel was tiny whereas Archer was large; she was sweet-tempered on the track as he was downright ruthless. What they shared was an impeccable pedigree for their occupation and a sad anticlimax to their lives. Unlikely a pair though they made, Archer and the Wheel captured the imagination of the racing public by coming as close to perfection on the track as has ever been witnessed. "What a mean-looking little devil," said Skylark about Wheel of Fortune in *The Illustrated Sporting and Dramatic News*.

"In her clothes there is really nothing remarkable about her except her apparent want of size and length but all these shortcomings, more apparent than real, disappear in a marvellously short space of time when Archer sets the mare a-going. Then she pulls herself out, lays herself down and makes the extremest use of every muscle and sinew; and be it noted she has not an atom of lumber about her. Wheel of Fortune's enormous propelling power is her grand character."

Wheel of Fortune was a bay by Adventurer out of Queen Bertha, the foundation mare of Lord Falmouth's Mereworth Stud in Kent. The latter ran indifferently as a juvenile in 1862, gaining only one decent victory at Newmarket in October, but the following year she won the Oaks by a head from Marigold at the rewarding odds of 40/1. "She started almost by a miracle," said a contemporary writer, "neglected by the public, held in no esteem by the owner and, at least a stone below her proper form, she snatched the race like a brand out of the fire." Queen Bertha proved the Oaks was no fluke by running second to Lord Clifden (the Derby second) in the St Leger and second to Macaroni (2,000 Guineas and Derby winner) in the Doncaster Cup within the space of 3 days. At Mereworth she bred 8 winners for Lord Falmouth. The fifth, by Macaroni, was Spinaway who won the 1,000 Guineas, Oaks, Nassau and Yorkshire Oaks of 1875 and then became the dam of Busybody who achieved the same classic double as her mother in 1884 after being sold at Lord Falmouth's dispersal sale for 8,800 guineas. Queen Bertha's 1875 visit to Adventurer, not much of a racehorse (he won the 1863 City & Suburban and Vase) but recently the sire of Pretender (2,000 Guineas and Derby) and the filly Apology, winner of the 1874 Triple Crown, resulted in the birth of her eighth winning offspring, namely Wheel of Fortune, the best racehorse Lord Falmouth ever owned.

Evelyn Boscawen, 6th Viscount Falmouth, came into the title unexpectedly upon the death of his cousin in 1852. His interest in the Turf dated

Wheel of Fortune (left), Atalanta (centre) dam of 1888 Derby winner Ayrshire and Mowerina (right) dam of 1889 Derby winner Donovan. All three with foals in the Welback paddocks, 1891

from 1857, initially under the name Mr T. Valentine, and his first 2 classic winners, Hurricane (1862 1,000 Guineas) and Queen Bertha were trained at Malton by John Scott. When he died in 1871 Falmouth sent his horses to Mat Dawson thereby inaugurating the triumvirate which saw his magpie colours of black jacket, white sleeves and red cap carried to innumerable successes, landing over £300,000 in stakes, until his withdrawal from racing at the end of the 1883 season. He never bet and was an immensely respected figure. However, Queen Bertha was the apple of his eye and a story is told that he bet Scott's wife sixpence that his mare would not win the Oaks and having lost the bet he presented her with the sixpence as a brooch set in diamonds. It was rumoured that he retired from racing because he suspected Archer of "pulling" his horse Galliard in the 1883 Derby but it is more likely that this move was primarily caused by advancing age and increasing ill-health. All bar four of Falmouth's 16 classic successes were partnered by Archer and 10 of them were gained by fillies.

The Wheel may have been small of stature but she was full to overflowing with character. She possessed the most remarkable constitution and was never sick or sorry nor refused a feed throughout the two seasons she was in training. This becomes all the more astounding when one considers the composition of her diet. She would dispose of a walnut or an orange with the greatest zeal and one evening even a couple of meat pies left in the corner of her box by her lad whilst he "did" the filly. They were twisted up in a paper bag but the Wheel soon nosed them out and, shaking them free, speedily disposed of the pair.

Lord Falmouth did not favour racing his two-year-olds early on. Consequently, though Wheel of Fortune was the sort to prosper in such circumstances she did not see a racecourse until Goodwood in July. Her trial took place at four in the morning and, ridden by Dawson's chief work rider Swift, she won as she liked. By 7a.m. she was on her way to Goodwood by special train. Wheel of Fortune's late arrival threw the market for the Richmond Stakes into total disarray but once it was known Archer had weighed-out to ride her the money poured in and she started a 2/1 on favourite.

The principal opposition was thought to lie with General Peel's colt Peter, also making his debut. However, the Wheel settled him right enough by 2 lengths. Peter was not beaten again during 1878 and wound up the season by carrying a 4lb penalty to victory in the Middle Park.

Wheel of Fortune's second outing was in York's Prince of Wales' Stakes in which she experienced some difficulty in shaking off Falmouth, winner of his 2 races to date. For the remainder of the season Archer merely had to point the filly in the right direction. No one opposed her for Doncaster's Wentworth Stakes and at Newmarket in the autumn she brought off a hat-trick in the Buckenham, Triennial Produce and Dewhurst Stakes. In the last named Wheel of Fortune "placed her backers on thorns for a few seconds", according to one reporter, but she won cleverly from Flavius in the end. Six races had netted £7,665 toward Falmouth's seasonal total of £38,000, a truly amazing sum for the period.

At the outset of the new season Mat Dawson's string numbered very nearly 100 horses, a figure smacking of 1979 rather than 1879, and included Lord Falmouth's five-year-olds Silvio (a Derby and St Leger winner), Il Gladiatore (Ebor) and Lady Golightly (placed in the 1,000 Guineas and St Leger), his four-year-olds Jannette (Oaks and St Leger) and Childeric (placed in the Derby and St Leger) besides the Wheel. "With such a wonderful lot of horses," said Dawson, "it was difficult to know how or when to run them in the weight-for-age races and, be it known, Lord Falmouth rarely stooped to handicaps." Given the fact that Falmouth never needed to know the "time of day" for betting purposes, his horses were seldom tried in the accepted sense of the word. In consequence they were always ready to do themselves justice and did not lose races they should have won due to overexertion on the trial grounds. In this context two trials in the spring of 1879 assume special significance.

In the first, which took place behind the Ditch, Wheel of Fortune failed to satisfy expectations. "This cannot be her right form," Dawson observed to his patron, "and if your lordship agrees we'll gallop the filly again next week." The second trial was over the full Rowley Mile and featured an astonishing array of talent. Four horses participated on strict weight-for-age terms – Silvio, Jannette, Wheel of Fortune and Charibert, a three-year-old colt who would win the 2,000 Guineas and Champion Stakes. Between them this quartet would collect 7 classics. "There's a sight, my lord," said Dawson, "the like of which you may never see again." Wheel of Fortune won the trial unextended and the 1,000 Guineas seemed a formality.

Only 7 accepted the challenge and some expressed surprise that the Wheel was allowed to start at odds as "long" as 75/40 on. Some money, however, was forthcoming for Reconciliation who had caused an upset by overturning Charibert at the previous Newmarket meeting, a performance looking all the better in the wake of the 2,000 Guineas result. Of course Archer knew how much Wheel of Fortune had in hand over Charibert and merely contented himself with allowing the great filly to lope home in a hack canter from Abbaye with Reconciliation a bad third. "A little big 'un on the shortest of legs and with the deepest girth imaginable," eulogised *The Illustrated Sporting and Dramatic News*, "we fear she will prove a spoilsport both in the Oaks and St Leger."

Wheel of Fortune encountered no problems whatsoever in fulfilling the

Coromandel II   Adventure   Wheel of Fortune.

The finish of the 1879 Oaks

first half of the prophesy. At Epsom she was faced by Philippine, who had been unbeaten as a juvenile, but she was not expected to stay the trip. Wheel of Fortune, starting at 3/1 on, the hottest favourite since Crucifix and the fourth shortest price in the history of the Oaks, was kept to the inside in typical Archer fashion throughout the entire race and simply hacked up. "Nothing could be more admirable than the Wheel's condition and she is a marvel of the *multum in parvo* class which she so worthily represents." Coromandel and Adventure filled the minor places. The Wheel's victory earned her dam immortality as the only Oaks heroine to breed two Oaks winners (Busybody's victory stretched the family sequence to an unparalleled three generations).

The Wheel's stiffest task came next, in the Prince of Wales' Stakes at Ascot, where she had to concede 16lb to Adventure and meet the colts Rayon d'Or (winner of the St James's Palace) and Ruperra with the worst of the weights. Accordingly, there was some opposition to her in the market and in the event she and Archer were pushed to beat Adventure $1\frac{1}{2}$ lengths with Rayon D'Or third. Nevertheless the merit of this performance can be gauged by the latter's subsequent victories in the Sussex, St Leger, Great Foal, Challenge and Champion Stakes.

A king's ransom began to pour on Wheel of Fortune for the St Leger now that she had displayed her mastery of the colts. Then disaster struck. The filly knocked herself at exercise and missed her Goodwood engagements, and Dawson expressed concern that she might not stand up to a full Leger preparation. It was decided to run her at York to assess her chances. On the Sunday before the Yorkshire Oaks she threw her lad at exercise, bolted and eventually slipped up. A foreleg began to fill. Dawson would not have sent her to York had she injured herself irrevocably but, by the same token, this incident could have done nothing to improve her well-being.

In the paddock she looked fit and walked soundly but Dawson took the precaution of bandaging both forelegs just the same. Archer kept her in rear for most of the $1\frac{1}{2}$ miles releasing her only within the last 100 yards. She won, pulling up, from Reconciliation.

So easy was her victory that Dawson, in consultation with Falmouth and Archer, decided to run her again 2 days later in the Great Yorkshire Stakes, a particularly risky policy with a filly who had been backed to win thousands in the St Leger if there were any misgivings about her legs taking the strain. One can only assume Dawson believed her sound. After a gallant struggle with Ruperra she succumbed by a length. Nothing but unflinching courage and determination could have got her so close for she pulled up hopelessly lame and Dawson's staff had the utmost difficulty getting her from the course to the railway station. Her dazzling career was at an end.

Ten victories from 11 starts yielded £19,740, a sum in 1879 surpassed among fillies only by her stablemate Jannette, and that from twice as many races.

There seemed every reason to expect that a classic-winning daughter of such a wonderful brood mare as Queen Bertha would prosper at stud. However, unlike her half-sister Spinaway, Wheel of Fortune did not flourish despite a promising start. Her first foal, a colt by Galopin called Oberon, won the Lincolnshire Handicap in 1887 by which date the Wheel had passed to the Duke of Portland as one of the choice lots in Falmouth's dispersal sale of June 30 1884. She made 5,000 guineas, 500 less than Spinaway, the entire sale of Falmouth's stock realizing £111,880.

With the stallion talent of Welbeck at his fingertips Portland gave Wheel of Fortune every opportunity to transmit her brilliance. Yet matings with sires of renown such as St Simon, Donovan and Carbine produced only one winner (Patria) for Portland before her death in November 1903, at the age of 27.

Archer had long since departed the world, mourned by owners, trainers, punters and public alike. Only the gods humbled the mighty combination of the Wheel and Fred Archer and they alone could defeat the great jockey, for as one poet declared:

> *Farewell best jockey ever seen on course;*
> *Thy backers weep to think by Fate's decree*
> *The rider pale upon his great white horse*
> *Hath beaten thee.*

WHEEL OF FORTUNE

Bay filly 1876
Ran 11   Won 10   Placed 1   Value of Races Won £19,740

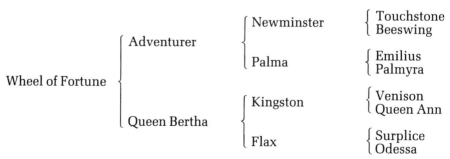

FOUR

Diadem and Steve Donoghue

"She was the strangest little creature that I ever rode. Before a race she was like a pony, so small, so insignificant, with nothing but her beautifully intelligent head to distinguish her." So spake Steve Donoghue in the spring of 1938 when asked to contemplate a riding career spanning nearly 40 years and assess the great horses he had partnered prior to facing the new challenge of training. The 10-times champion jockey, successful in 14 classics, had been quick to respond. Brown Jack was his favourite, Humorist the gamest, Gay Crusader the best, Tishy the slowest and Ramus the most difficult. However, in Donoghue's opinion, by far the sweetest was Lord d'Abernon's little chestnut mare Diadem whom he partnered to 13 victories between 1919 and 1921. Once mounted and cantering to post Diadem's whole demeanour began to alter:

"All her lassitude and quietness disappeared and she grew in stature so that from the saddle she seemed like a 16 hands horse full of mettle and vitality. Once facing the tapes with her head turned for home she was all life and fire and one could feel every muscle in her body taut and strung up for the contest, and she would watch for the tapes to go up and then spring forward through them with the speed of a catapult loosed from a sling. Whatever the distance she ran the race out to the finish, dead game. It was thrilling to feel the sheer pluck with which she responded but I hated giving so courageous a little creature hard races. It was her misfortune to be so good that she was usually giving weight away."

Docility and spirit were just two of Diadem's qualities. She was also exceptionally durable, running 39 times over 6 seasons, a strenuous career for a 1,000 Guineas winner and Oaks second, credentials that would consign many a filly straight to stud. During a career of this length she necessarily encountered more than one jockey but according to her trainer George Lambton the identity of her personal favourite was beyond question: Steve Donoghue.

> "I've seen her after a hard race, as he unsaddled her, turn round and rub her nose against his hands more like a dog than a horse. Stephen is a great lover of horses but I am sure Diadem held first place in his affections and she thoroughly reciprocated it. Win or lose you could not have made Stephen hit her for anything in the world."

Donoghue detested the whip (and in fact D'Abernon insisted that in no circumstances should Diadem ever be struck), considering it the last resort because "9 times out of 10 when the time comes to think of the whip the race is lost and no purpose is served by using it". His preferences lent toward tender treatment incorporating silk-smooth hands, a talent which drew one rival jockey to declare that Donoghue could discover more about a horse's reserves "with his little finger than most men with their legs and whip". One day at Doncaster Donoghue rode Diadem with one hand useless owing to a broken wrist yet the partnership still prevailed by a short head. Donoghue genuinely loved all horses and this affection found no finer recipient than Diadem.

Diadem was bred by her owner Lord D'Abernon, formerly Sir Edgar Vincent, from his good race mare Donnetta whom he purchased for 450 guineas. D'Abernon did not subscribe to the view that mares should automatically be retired at three or four years of age. Donnetta won Kempton's big races, the Jubilee and Duke of York, and raced till she was eight thereby setting a precedent for her most famous daughter. She had already foaled the useful sprinter/miler Diadumenos, winner of the Jubilee and Liverpool Cup, by Orby when a second mating with the Derby winner produced Diadem in 1914. A subsequent colt foal by Orby's Derby winning son Grand Parade, called Diophon, won the 1924 2,000 Guineas in the colours of the Aga Khan.

D'Abernon was convinced Diadem was the best he had ever bred, an opinion received with some scepticism by Lambton when he first clapped eyes on the filly.

> "She was a small dark chestnut, rather light of bone, with a light neck and apparently without much energy but she had a beautiful intelligent head and did everything that was asked of her without any fuss or bother. Still I could not see where her great excellence was to come from."

However, Lambton respected his owner's judgement and he determined to take more than an ordinary interest in Diadem. Through the winter and spring of 1916 she worked satisfactorily without showing any particular merit but being late in her coat and rather a shy feeder, she was not ready

Diadem and Steve Donoghue

to run before the Coventry Stakes, which owing to the war was run at Newmarket instead of Ascot. In a rough gallop 10 days before the race Diadem showed Lambton that D'Abernon had not overestimated her ability and despite giving a passable imitation of an old sheep in the preliminaries, won the Coventry by two lengths.

The war naturally restricted Diadem's activities. After the Coventry she won 3 of her remaining 4 races as a juvenile, losing the Hopeful Stakes after being badly interfered with at the gate. These 5 rides were shared between the American "Skeets" Martin and Fred Rickaby and it was the latter who partnered Diadem to her ½-length victory over Sunny Jane in the 1,000 Guineas of 1917. Diadem then took her chance in the Derby since Lambton and D'Abernon held no exalted opinion of the favourite Gay Crusader because he had struggled to beat one of the stable's lesser lights in the Column Produce Stakes. The possibility of the extra ½-mile exposing Diadem's stamina was compounded by torrential rain and once Lambton saw how much physical improvement Gay Crusader had made since the

Column Produce he knew the filly's task was hopeless. In the circumstances Rickaby gave her an easy race when victory proved out of the question because there was still the Oaks to aim for. However, the incessant rain churned the course into a sea of mud and even Diadem's brave heart could not cope with 2 tough contests over this distance in such a brief space of time. Sunny Jane reversed Guineas form to win by $\frac{1}{2}$ length.

Lambton put his filly away till the autumn when she reappeared to win twice from 3 starts over sprint distances in the hands of Rickaby. The following season the Australian Brownie Carslake took over the reins (Rickaby was serving in the Tank Corps and was sadly killed in action) and he partnered Diadem to 3 consecutive victories, including a magnificent effort under 9st 8lb in the Salford Borough Handicap, before Albert Whalley rode her into third place in the Champion Stakes. In 3 seasons Diadem's record stood at 10 wins from 15 races and she had been associated with 4 jockeys. Then, on May 10th 1919 in Hurst Park's Victoria Cup, she was introduced to Steve Donoghue and all bar 2 of her remaining 24 races were in his tender care, 13 of them victorious. Only Joe Childs, in the Cambridgeshire of 1919, and George Colling, in the walkover for the 1920 July Cup (Donoghue rode at Worcester for his friend Jimmy White) interrupted this sequence which ended at Royal Ascot on June 16th 1921 with the Rous Memorial. Many mares become highly strung and are incapable of reproducing their best after a second summer in training, but not Diadem. She maintained her great courage and placid temperament right to that very last day at Ascot. D'Abernon risked public censure (and forfeited lucrative sums for her progeny) by keeping her in training so long but he realized an owner cannot expect a Diadem in his string every year and as long as she was fit and happy he was not about to forego the pleasure of watching her in action.

Ever since the day Donoghue tamed a bucking donkey during a visit by Ohmy's Circus to his home town of Warrington he had been consumed by a passion for horses. He idolized the stylish American rider Tod Sloan who, it was alleged, got the best from his mounts by whispering sweet nuthins in their ears, and he determined to follow in his footsteps by riding winners in all the great races. After learning his trade with John Porter (he only lasted 4 months), Dobson Peacock and Alfred Sadler, Donoghue perfected his technique with spells under Edward Johnson in France and Michael Dawson in Ireland. He returned to England in 1911 to ride for Atty Persse and immediately made his name as the rider of The Tetrarch, unbeaten in 7 races as a two-year-old in 1913.

The Donoghue–Diadem team did not get off to a winning start in the Victoria Cup. The mare looked dull in her coat and had not yet come to herself. But in seven further outings during 1919 they were only beaten once, and that in truly sensational circumstances at Goodwood. A return to the normal racing calendar also saw Diadem visit Royal Ascot for the first time, winning the first and last races at the meeting. She took the 7-furlong Rous Memorial in hollow fashion by 6 lengths and in the Kings Stand, run in a downpour on the Friday, gave 21lb and a 2-length beating to Best Born. Next time out Diadem galloped her solitary opponent Iron Hand into the ground to win the 6-furlong July Cup, but Liverpool's Molyneux Plate on July 24th proved a different proposition altogether.

Burdened with 9st 7lb Diadem was 7/4 favourite to beat a field of crack sprint handicappers and as usual did not impress on the way to post. However, approaching the distance she closed on the long-time leader Trogon and responded gamely to Donoghue's exhortations to pass him and then withstand a last-ditch challenge from Pandion. "A fine performance by Diadem is feature of the second day," commented The Sporting Life. Six days later Diadem headed for Goodwood's King George Stakes, then the most valuable conditions race for sprinters in the calendar. Four opposed her and she lobbed down to the start, just beyond the brow of the hill, a red-hot 5/2 on favourite. When the race got underway minutes later and the field came in view of the stands Diadem could be seen some 20 lengths adrift. The filly Chiffre d'Amour won easily and Donoghue brought the favourite back to a torrent of abuse from the betting public. An enquiry was promptly called and the stewards took the unprecedented step of convening it on the open verandah outside the stewards' room. For 25 minutes Donoghue endured the comments of a howling mob who had no idea of events at the start which precipitated Diadem's misfortune. The actual culprit, and rightful target for the crowd's wrath, was Sun d'Or who whipped sideways as the tapes rose and carried Diadem and poor Donoghue off to the left. Donoghue was exonerated but the distraught jockey still felt obliged to seek out his faithful partner immediately afterwards. "I felt certain the little mare realized our troubles and could sympathise," he wrote. "She always seemed to understand every word I said to her."

The partnership soon resumed its winning ways. A trip to Ireland annexed the £1,275 Curragh Plate, the richest sprint Diadem ever won, under 10st 2lb and conceding the runner-up 30lb; the Town Moor Handicap, under 9st 12lb, was won by a head in concession of 24lb to Quadrille and her single rival in the Challenge Stakes constituted no problem whatsoever. The second leg of this hat-trick was especially memorable since Donoghue ought not to have ridden at Doncaster at all. This was the occasion when he rode Diadem with a strapped-up broken wrist. "She seemed to know that I was injured for she helped me in every way. She was carrying a great weight and it was a fast-run race but she did everything and I won a grand

Diadem winning the 1919 Molyneux Plate at Liverpool

race with one hand."

Diadem's fourth season concluded with second place in the Cambridge-shire (ridden by Joe Childs) where she failed to concede 30lb to the ligh-tweight Brigand. She needed one race in 1920 (second in Newbury's Empire Stakes to Golden Orb, trying to give him 31lb) to prepare for Royal Ascot, a meeting which arguably comprised the high watermark of her entire career, since she collected no less than three prizes, a feat seldom attempted this century and standing only beside names like The Earl (1868), Lowlander (1874), Verneuil (1878), Tristan (1882), Galliard (1883) and Hornets Beauty (1911). Admittedly the Rous Memorial was a walkover after the 21 other names on the racecard decided to seek easier competition but Diadem's victories in the All-Aged and Kings Stand were worthy of any royal fixture. Starting odds-on in each case Donoghue brought her home by 6 lengths from Tetrameter in the former and by 4 lengths from Dissolved in the Kings Stand. The crowd roared their approval of an historic achievement.

Although the partnership won more races, that June Friday signalled the last great victory for all Diadem's best subsequent performances came in defeat. She took the Bottisham Plate (conceding 40lb to the second) and July Cup (walkover) at Newmarket but lost both her mid-summer targets, the Molyneux and King George, albeit covering herself in glory in the process.

The weather at Liverpool resembled mid-winter rather than mid-summer. Temperatures demanded overcoats and rain had been falling in buckets all week. Diadem had 9st 9lb to carry through these arctic conditions, a fearful enough task in the first instance which became virtually impossible once the Irish mare Tut Tut had interfered with her at the tapes. However, Donoghue gathered her together and patiently made up his ground to challenge the winner, Racket (7st 11lb) but the weight difference inevitably held sway and two lengths still divided them at the post.

Glorious Goodwood presented an equally bleak façade that summer of 1920. Rain, and even sleet, sluiced down topped by a bitterly cold wind that blew from the stands side right across the course. The 6-furlongs King George Stakes was reduced to a match between Diadem and the three-year-old Tetratema, the undefeated winner of the National Breeders, Champagne, Imperial Produce and Middle Park as a juvenile and runner-up in the 2,000 Guineas. Having failed to stay in the Derby, he reverted to sprinting with a victory in Ascot's Fern Hill Stakes, and would receive 8lb from Diadem on the weight-for-age scale.

Unfortunately for little Diadem she was drawn on the stands side and thus screened her rival from the worst of the elements. For 5 pulsating furlongs the pair hammered away at each other until the mare finally cracked. Carslake, who rode Tetratema, recalled Diadem's tenacity from that day at Manchester and after the race admitted to Lambton that he had been somewhat apprehensive about the result as they passed the furlong marker since Tetratema had not one ounce left to give. Donoghue took no credit for himself. "In the last 50 yards she seemed to simply hurl herself forward in a final effort to beat her rival. It was the most gallant attempt on the part of an animal I have ever known."

In many respects this tremendous exertion finished Diadem. Her conqueror went on to win a Kings Stand, July Cup and another King George. It was no disgrace at 6 years of age to be beaten by a rising champion. "If youth, as usual prevailed," said *The Sporting Life*, "Diadem failed gloriously."

A walkover at Newmarket and a facile success in a $1\frac{1}{2}$-mile race at Kempton Park (they went no gallop and played into the sprinter's hands) prefaced another abortive attack on the Champion Stakes. Ironically for such a tremendous sprinter Diadem's 24th and last victory was her only one over $1\frac{1}{2}$ miles.

Lord D'Abernon kept Diadem in training with the intention of winning a third Rous Memorial and equalling Hornets Beauty's Royal Meeting record of 6 victories, after which she would be retired. She and Donoghue (later to win seven on Brown Jack) could not quite accomplish their objective. After a pipe-opener at Epsom, in which she carried 10 stone, Diadem's near-fore joint began to give Lambton cause for concern. His fears increased alarmingly when the ground at Ascot was seen to be terribly hard. Lambton contemplated withdrawing her but she moved so freely in her final piece of work that he advised Lord D'Abernon to let her run.

On entering the paddock to see Diadem saddled Mrs Lambton discovered that she had lost her brooch. This was no ordinary brooch for it comprised the mare's name outlined in diamonds and had been given her by Lord D'Abernon after Diadem's first victory in 1916. Ever since the Coventry, Mrs Lambton had worn the brooch at all Diadem's races as a lucky charm. Not wishing to accept the portent she kept the news from her husband till after the race when the accuracy of this omen was proven all too apparent. Diadem was beaten 2 lengths by Monarch and pulled up very sore, not on the near-fore, but as is invariably the case, protecting the weak leg put too much pressure on the other. The brooch was never recovered.

One of the most romantic partnerships in Turf history had come to an end. Although Donoghue later developed another enduring relationship with Brown Jack his attachment to Diadem remained unbroken. He later wrote:

> "Dear little Diadem, the gamest and sweetest-tempered animal that any one could possibly imagine. She wanted nothing more than a kind word whispered in her ear at the crucial moment and she would strain every nerve in her body. If ever I rode a champion it was Diadem."

Diadem was put down aged 17 in June 1931 after producing just five foals of whom the filly Dian won over £4,000. Though her influence upon the modern thoroughbred therefore could never be substantial her name lives on via the 6-furlong Pattern race run at Ascot every September, much as her friend Steve Donoghue's does at Epsom, to remind us of a true gem in racing's crown.

DIADEM

Chestnut filly 1914
Ran 39   Won 24   Placed 11   Value of Races Won £16,058

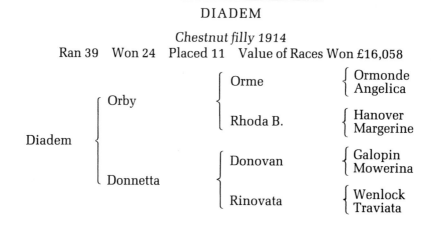

FIVE

Sun Chariot and Gordon Richards

Gordon Richards' status as the outstanding British jockey of the first half, if not all, of the 20th century rests not only upon the sheer statistics of his career but also a character of the utmost integrity and honesty.

Records he broke at will, most of them Fred Archer's. He was champion 26 times in the 29 years between 1925 and 1953, easily surpassing Fordham's total of 14 and Archer's 13; he rode 4,870 winners from 21,843 mounts (beating Archer's 2,749 on April 26th 1943), including a record 269 in 1947 and a record 12 consecutive winners in October 1933 (he initially took Archer's seasonal best of 246 in 1933); and he won 14 classics, a figure some way behind Piggott, Buckle and Archer, however.

In the Derby his bad luck was legendary until Pinza, his 28th and final ride, proved successful in 1953. In both 1938 and 1940 he partnered the wrong one of Fred Darling's two horses whilst in 1941 he missed the ride on Owen Tudor due to a broken leg.

A short, stocky miner's son from Shropshire possessing a shock of thick black hair that earned him the nickname of "Moppy" as a youth, Richards was inspired by a single-minded determination to ride as many winners as he possibly could and 12 of his championships were won with totals exceeding 200 (Archer managed eight), a feat virtually unheard of in the years since his retirement despite the proliferation of evening fixtures.

His style of riding was far from classic. He rode his finishes on a loose rein and was apt to twist his body round in the saddle in a manner reminiscent of Fordham. Like the inimitable Piggott perch of more recent years this unique style would have earned an apprentice severe censure. All the same, he could hold horses together just with his legs and they ran as straight as a gun barrel for him. At the gate, where he was invariably the fastest away, and in a finish, where he never accepted defeat until the winning post was reached, he was faultless. In the former situation many jockeys were convinced the starter never released the tapes unless Gordon had announced his readiness but there could be no grouses concerning his power in a finish. "You'd go alongside him to challenge," said 5 times champion Doug Smith, "and think maybe you were going to pass, then he'd pull a little extra out and keep his horse going until the post." Two other great men of the Turf put Richards' genius in a nutshell. Lord Rosebery observed that he surely lost fewer races he ought to have won than any other jockey while the Aga Khan was even more to the point: "He has the will to win."

Gordon Richards needed all these talents at his disposal when he made the acquaintance of Sun Chariot in the spring of 1942. Though she won 3 classics that season to stand alongside Sceptre and Pretty Polly as one of the brilliant race mares of the 20th century, she still contrived to pose innumerable problems to a jockey as redoubtable as Richards. He said of her:

> "She was a machine, and what a character. I've a few grey hairs and she gave them to me. She was probably the greatest racehorse I've ever been across. You never knew what she would do. In the Oaks she let them go a furlong at the start; then decided to go after them and won in a canter. In the St Leger she made a hack of the Derby winner. She was only defeated once but should never have been beaten."

On other occasions Richards chose to bracket her name with Pinza's but on the subject of Sun Chariot's character he remained unequivocal, "She was a monkey!"

The presence of numerous unstable influences among Sun Chariot's recent ancestors might account for her wayward streak. Her sire Hyperion was a sweet-natured little horse in spite of being inbred 4×3 to St Simon and numbering the fiery father and daughter combination of Tristan (who killed himself in a fit of temper by banging his head against the wall of his box) and Canterbury Pilgrim among his forbears. There was more St Simon blood on the distaff side of Sun Chariot's pedigree, albeit a little further removed, via Persimmon, a great-grandparent of her dam Clarence. Moreover, Clarence, who never ran, was by Diligence whose grandam Cheshire Cat was the matriarch of a family noted for misbehaviour. On the credit side, Clarence's dam Nun's Veil was a precociously fast two-year-old who won 3 times and coincidentally ran second to Hyperion in the New Stakes. Besides Sun Chariot, Clarence bred Calash (a full sister) who became the dam of 1957 Oaks winner Carrozza, and Sister Clara, the grandam of 1964 Derby winner Santa Claus. In short, ability just about balanced potential mischief in Sun Chariot's family tree.

Sun Chariot was bred at the National Stud which, in 1939, was based

Sun Chariot, November 1942 by Sir Alfred Munnings

at Tully in County Kildare, and leased to King George VI in company with Big Game, a fine, powerful-looking (though in actuality none too robust) colt by Bahram. Both animals duly crossed the Irish Sea to join the King's other horses at Fred Darling's Beckhampton stable on the Wiltshire Downs. An irascible martinet of the old school, Darling nevertheless was a trainer of whom employees, owners and commentators were unanimous in their praise. By the time of Sun Chariot's arrival Darling had collected 4 of his 6 trainers' championships and won 12 classics. Before his death, just after Pinza's Derby, he had added a further 7 classics to that total, 4 of them from Big Game and Sun Chariot. Yet even a master trainer like Darling was almost fooled by Sun Chariot's antics in the beginning, for she worked so discouragingly that he decided to return her to Ireland. Luckily for Darling, wartime restrictions on the movement of horses necessitated the issue of an export licence and thanks to bureaucratic delay, Sun Chariot had begun to serve notice that she did indeed possess more than a grain of talent by the day it arrived. Therefore instead of a boat voyage to Ireland, Sun Chariot, or the Clarence filly as she was still titled, took a box-ride to Newbury for the 5-furlong Acorn Plate on June 6th.

Sun Chariot won this race comfortably, much as she did her remaining 3 outings in the Queen Mary, Amesbury (Salisbury) and Middle Park Stakes.

The first-named was run at Newmarket as a substitute for the normal Royal Ascot race. Owing to the war Sun Chariot would only compete at 3 venues. Although Big Game won substitute races for the Coventry and Champagne Stakes, Sun Chariot's three-length victory from Ujiji in the Middle Park (the first by a filly since Golden Corn in 1921) earned her premier position in the Free Handicap with 9st 7lb, one pound more than her stable companion.

The filly had accomplished all this without Richards. He was leading the jockeys' table with 22 winners on May 1st when a horse lashed out down at the Salisbury start and struck him above the left ankle, terminating his season. Consequently Harry Wragg, who eventually took the jockeys' title with 71 winners, partnered Sun Chariot throughout her juvenile career.

Richards sat with his leg in plaster listening to the wireless description of Billy Nevett's successful substitution on Owen Tudor in the Derby (and Wragg's on Commotion in the Oaks) wondering whether the 1942 season would see him return to his best.

At first it did not seem that he was. Sun Chariot's reappearance was in Salisbury's Southern Stakes on April 25th by which date Richards had not ridden a winner. Naturally the royal filly looked a banker for him but, unlike the public, he knew what a terror she had been at Beckhampton where she habitually imitated one of her royal predecessors, the St Simon colt Diamond Jubilee. In between trying to bite his jockey or standing on his hind legs, Diamond Jubilee won the Prince of Wales a Triple Crown in 1900. The only member of the human race receiving the Diamond's approval was his lad Herbert Jones who, wisely, was eventually entrusted with the ride on him in the classics. In similar vein Sun Chariot responded best to her devoted lad G. Warren who more often as not rode her at exercise. However, she continued to perplex Richards. "She would not start and kept on going round in rings when you wanted to get her away. You never knew whether or not you were going to get to the top of the gallop." With his self-confidence undermined and having to take on trust Sun Chariot's willingness to co-operate, Richards was on a hiding to nothing.

Darling instructed him to give Sun Chariot a chance in the race by dropping her in behind the leaders in the hope she might settle. Sun Chariot soon showed who was the boss, refusing to take any interest in the proceedings. Suffice to say she finished a poor third, several lengths behind Ujiji whom she had trounced in the Middle Park. There and then Richards decided that Sun Chariot must be left to her own devices if she were to put her best foot forward. She repaid him by trotting-up at the next Salisbury meeting over 7 furlongs.

The winners had begun to flow again for Richards but as the 1,000 Guineas

approached he was no nearer unravelling the mystery of Sun Chariot's personality. Particularly worrying was her attitude at the starting gate. "She
gave you a nasty feeling going in, always behind her bridle, with her head
round on one side looking at you." In her final gallop she was especially
obstreperous. Furthermore, the Guineas was to be run on the 13th!

Richards' worries proved groundless. Boosted by a 4-length success on
Big Game in the 2,000 the previous afternoon, he steered Sun Chariot
through the preliminaries without too much consternation (she needed a
lead before consenting to go down the course and swished her tail persis-
tently) and apart from trying to look round once or twice she won as she
liked by 4 lengths from Perfect Peace. Her time of 1 minute 39.6 seconds
was 1.2 seconds faster than that of Big Game.

*Sun Chariot and Gordon Richards – a fine shot of her swishing her tail in
petulance before the 1,000 Guineas*

The filly had grown into an imposing animal, not very tall at 15.2¼ hands, but possessing plenty of scope and enormous power through her back and hind quarters. Yet her convoluted psyche was still all too obvious. The morning the King and Queen visited Beckhampton to see Sun Chariot work before the Oaks loses nothing in the retelling.

In the circumstances of a royal visit Richards, not Warren, was instructed to ride Sun Chariot. It is impossible to say for certain whether separation from her trusted human companion provoked the events which followed but it's a thought nonetheless. Sun Chariot refused to budge and when Templeton, Darling's head-lad, went behind her and administered a tap with his hunting crop she carted Richards into a ploughed field where she dropped to her knees and began roaring like a bull. "I have seen a colt do this but I had never seen a filly do it and I don't want to again," Richards wrote afterwards. "Eventually she did decide to go but we had a tremendous tussle with her that morning."

Sun Chariot, however, was as tough as old boots and could absorb anything Darling or Richards cared to throw at her. Neither the distance nor the opposition posed the slightest danger to her in the Oaks. Only her volcanic temperament lay between Sun Chariot and a second facile classic success.

All 5 classics in 1942 were run on Newmarket's July Course where the 1½-mile start is behind the plantation and therefore not visible from the grandstand. Just as well for the King and Queen's peace of mind because Sun Chariot gave a delinquent performance of virtuoso proportions. Three times she thwarted the starter. At the fourth attempt she was at least facing the right way and he let them go. Richards was then obliged to live out his recurring nightmare for as the tapes rose Sun Chariot ducked away to the left with the royal jockey a helpless passenger. "The field must have gone a furlong before I had covered much more than 50 yards."

All this drama had passed unnoticed. When the spectators in the stands got their first glimpse of the field approaching the turn into the straight the 4/1-on favourite could be seen gaining ground hand over fist on the wide outside. For some unaccountable reason Sun Chariot had now decided to race and Richards was not about to risk breaking the spell. "She was going so well that I decided to let her canter on – no more Salisbury disasters through interfering with this wayward miss." Three furlongs out Sun Chariot collared the leaders and, though relaxing once she struck the front, resisted a challenge from Afterthought by a length. "It's a relief, now it's all over," Richards told pressmen. "You simply don't know what she will do but there is no doubt of her ability."

Big Game failed to stay sufficiently well to win the Derby, thereby ensuring the filly would represent the King in the St Leger on September 12th (Big

Game won the Champion Stakes instead). In preparation for Sun Chariot's sternest examination Darling arranged for her to use the 1¾-mile Barton gallop at Joe Lawson's Manton establishment not far from Beckhampton. Three other horses participated in the gallop, Botree (borrowed from George Todd) and the filly's 2 customary workmates, her lead horse Massowa and the useful four-year-old stayer Bakhtawar. Richards rode the latter with the faithful Warren aboard Sun Chariot. Without a race for nearly 3 months it was essential Sun Chariot be tested to the full. After Botree and Massowa had cut out the pace for 9 furlongs, Richards pushed Bakhtawar ahead but only on suffrance. A furlong from the end of the gallop Sun Chariot ranged alongside, pulling Warren's arms out. Away she went, leaving Beckhampton in no doubt that the St Leger was theirs for the taking, even more so after Bakhtawar (under 9st 2lb) was just beaten a short head and a head by Afterthought and High Table in the Jockey Club Cup on the day preceding the Leger. In the gallop Sun Chariot had given Bakhtawar 7lb and beaten him half a furlong.

The well-muscled appearance of Watling Street and the excellent recent form of his stable combined to make the Derby winner 2/1 favourite with Sun Chariot at 9/4. The irony of what followed was consequently not lost on the cognoscenti. In the parade Sun Chariot behaved like a novice nun whilst Watling Street, who had begun to terrorise the Newmarket gallops, frequently bucked and kicked. The improvement in Sun Chariot's behaviour, a characteristic of many fillies as autumn approaches, was further reflected in the race itself. Watling Street was the horse playing up at the start. The filly, by contrast, behaved impeccably and, tucked in at the rear of the 8 runners, tracked Watling Street when he made his effort ½ mile from home. At the merest sign from her jockey Sun Chariot swept by imperiously to crush the colt by 3 lengths with the Derby second Hyperides a further 5 lengths behind in third place. "They never really saw the way she went," according to Richards who had no doubt at all that had Sun Chariot run in the Derby "she would have won that just as easily".

Seldom is a Derby winner so comprehensively defeated by a filly in the St Leger and it was somewhat surprising to find Sun Chariot only coupled with Big Game at the top of the three-year-old Free Handicap, albeit 3lb his superior once the sex adjustment had been made. She was a much better horse than that, one to rank with the greatest of her sex. The same cannot be said of Big Game.

Wartime limited Sun Chariot's earnings to £9,208 from eight victories yet she conclusively proved superior to the colts of her generation at two and three years of age. Despite another 12 years in the saddle Gordon Richards never rode another filly who rivalled Sun Chariot's brilliance and

Nearing the finish of the 1942 Oaks, Sun Chariot on the right

possibly only one colt who equalled it. Association with a mare like Sun Chariot was certainly worth a few grey hairs.

SUN CHARIOT

Brown filly 1939
Ran 9   Won 8   Placed 1   Value of Races Won £9,208

Sun Chariot	Hyperion	Gainsborough	Bayardo
			Rosedrop
		Selene	Chaucer
			Serenissima
	Clarence	Diligence	Hurry on
			Ecurie
		Nun's Veil	Friar Marcus
			Blanche

SIX

Busher and John Longden

The American public, weaned on a pioneering spirit which lionises the conquest of adversity in all its forms, demands true grit of its heroes. From Davy Crockett to George Patton the American hero is imbued with guts. Moreover, for every Crockett there was an Annie Oakley or Calamity Jane, because to many Americans the national character derived from the stalwart womenfolk who provided the backbone to daily life on the frontier. America views its equine heroes and heroines no differently. Generally speaking they race more often than their European counterparts and the odd defeat is seen as no cause for idols to be shattered. In the 1945 season, as a far costlier national triumph was dawning, the American racing public warmed to a combination packed with guts and determination, the three-year-old filly Busher and her 38-year-old rider John Longden.

Longden typified the American dream. One of 6 children born to a Wakefield miner he arrived in America in April 1912 as a five-year-old boy. Unbeknown to young Longden he had already scored one victory over adversity because had he and his mother Mary (father Herbert had preceded them to set up home) not missed their train to Liverpool they would have journeyed third-class on the *Titanic*! Instead of an almost certain watery grave the remaining Longdens enjoyed a safe crossing on the *Virginian*.

Their new home was Tabor, a Mormon community in Alberta, where Herbert Longden, a member of the faith, could also obtain work in the mines. At the age of 13 John would follow his father. To the slice of luck which actually got him to America in the first place Longden now bonded a toughness of body and soul. For a wage of one penny-farthing a day he became a grease-pig, greasing the wheels of the trucks carrying coal to the surface, while indulging in plenty of overtime digging the coal itself. Although standing a tiny 4 feet 11 inches this heavy work bequeathed a strong pair of shoulders and forearms which he put to good use as an ice-hockey player. However, Longden saw his future elsewhere.

"I'd been reading all the books I could find about racing, horses and jockeys and it was strongly in my mind that some day I could be a jockey. I was the right size for it. Sure it was a kid's dream then, but if you make up your mind about something, think about it long enough, become determined it will be a reality, then you've got a fighting chance it will happen."

Longden rode his first winner on Rainbow at Tabor County Fair in 1924, a 4-furlong dash, bareback. After years honing his skills on the county fair circuit, often riding in Roman races (balancing between two barebacked horses, one foot on each) and supplementing his income by competing in running races, bronc-busting, trick-riding or mine work plus the occasional foray to Cuba and the other Mormon community of Salt Lake City, where on October 4th, 1927 he rode his first official winner on an unreliable animal called Hugo K. Asher, Longden began to fulfil those mineshaft dreams. Winners accumulated at places such as Winnipeg and Calgary and he became known as the "King of the half-milers". In the fall of 1931 his thoughts turned to California and Johnny Longden was on his way.

When Longden mounted Busher for the first time on May 26th, 1945 at Santa Anita racetrack in California he had over 2,000 winners to his credit, including a Triple Crown on Count Fleet, and had been champion jockey in 1938. He had also experienced some crashing falls. In 1935 one left him paralysed from the waist down (not for the last time he was told he would never ride again) and in July 1944 he took another spectacular spill from the filly Dine and Dance at Empire City. A piece of paper blew across the track spooking the filly who ran into the rail. Longden went down and was trampled. He came out of it with a badly broken foot, insufficient to stop him driving Fast Fiddle to a head victory in the following day's Butler Handicap. The next morning Longden could not get out of bed, not because of the foot but due to severe back pains. An X-ray showed he had ridden with two fractured vertebrae! "I began to have doubts about ever riding again after that bad spill. They had been calling me an old man even before this." Just when a fillip was vital he received a phone call from George Odom, trainer to film mogul Louis B. Mayer, offering him a stable retainer. Longden accepted the deal and thus became associated with Busher, "the greatest of her sex I had anything to do with".

Busher was foaled on April 27th, 1942 at the Idle Hour Stock Farm of Colonel Edward Riley Bradley in Fayette County, Lexington, Kentucky. Ultimately growing to 16 hands she was repeatedly described as decidedly "masculine" in her make-up, an accusation often levelled at fillies who prove capable of taking on and beating the colts, which Busher accomplished five times during 1945. Seldom are three-year-old fillies pitched against the colts

Busher and John Longden

in American racing but Busher proved more than equal to the task. "She wasn't really feminine at all," says Longden.

"She was compact and heavily muscled with tremendously powerful quarters on her. She had blistering speed and you could place her wherever you wanted to and she was as honest as the day is long."

The jockey would have cause to be thankful for these characteristics in addition to the filly's intelligent, placid disposition. In motion, Busher drew all the superlatives. "She is one of the smoothest and most easy-gaited of runners," concluded the *American Racing Manual*, "appearing to glide or float over the ground without exertion. She increases or decreases her speed imperceptibly and her gameness is absolute."

Bradley bred her to combine class with durability, for she came from the European classic-winning family of La Troienne while her sire War Admiral, a Triple Crown winner himself, was a son of "Big Red", the immortal Man o' War, the "mostest hoss dat ever wuz" in the words of his devoted groom Will Harbut.

Considered good enough by her breeder Marcel Boussac to run in the French 1,000 Guineas, La Troienne was purchased by Bradley for 1,250 guineas at the Newmarket December Sales of 1930. He bred 10 winners from her, 5 of stakes calibre. The best of these were Black Helene who won the Coaching Club American Oaks, American Derby and Florida Derby, Bimelech who won the Preakness and Belmont in 1940 and Big Hurry, a fast juvenile of 1938 who won the Selima Stakes and became the great grandam of Allez France. Other notable members of this family are Buckpasser, Personality and Dapper Dan.

La Troienne's filly foal by Bradley's 1926 Kentucky Derby winner Bubbling Over was named Baby League and though she only scored once on the track she bred nine winners, one of whom was Busher. From Baby League's other daughters descend such performers as Boucher (1972 St Leger) and Numbered Account, the champion American filly of 1971.

The Bradley mares were invariably mated with his own stallions and he deliberately avoided using any sire possessing Fair Play blood, which he regarded as temperamentally unsuitable. This, of course, precluded the use of even as great a horse as Fair Play's son Man o' War and it was not until the emergence of War Admiral that Bradley revised his policy toward this male line. One of the first results of this change of mind was Busher. Significantly she carried the coat not of her sire (brown) or her dam (bay) but of her paternal grandsire – a rich golden chestnut, disrupted only by a small pointed star on her forehead.

To begin with Busher failed to distinguish herself. She was small, and in early training trials displayed a poor action which boded ill for her juvenile campaign of 1944. Nevertheless she proceeded to win 4 of her 6 starts at Belmont, between May 30th and September 13th, in the hands of Eddie Arcaro. The 2 defeats she suffered to Price Level and Nomadic were handsomely avenged in the last of these 6 races, the $22,530 Matron Stakes over 6 furlongs. Busher capped her season by travelling south to collect Laurel Park's even more valuable ($25,780) Selima Stakes over $1\frac{1}{16}$ mile in which she comfortably defeated Gallorette (later to challenge her own popularity and sustained level of track performance with a career total of 21 victories which broke Busher's stakes record for a filly with $445,535) and Ace Card who would win the Pimlico and Delaware Oaks. Thus the unconsidered youngster had won 5 of her 7 races, and made enough of an impact to attract the attention of Louis B. Mayer who paid $50,000 for her on March 23rd 1945.

Longden's partnership with Busher began with 5 races at the 6-week Santa Anita festival during May and July. They won 4 of them. The first 2, confined to fillies, were annexed by the contemptuous margins of 5 lengths and 7 lengths. However, the following 2 races, the San Vincente Handicap and the Santa Anita Derby, involved confrontation with colts. Busher won the former handily enough but after the Santa Anita Derby Longden discovered just how uncompromising a taskmaster Mayer could be. "He couldn't take defeat. He got very upset when Busher was beaten by Bymeabond in the Derby," says Longden before adding honestly:

"Well he was right. That was my fault. I gave her a bad ride. I made the wrong move with her and got carried to the outside. The other horse got through on the inside and took us. It never should have happened."

The race did appear to lie at Busher's mercy entering the straight but, although finishing strongly, in running so wide she could not repel the colt who had railed like a greyhound. Eleven days later Busher completed her Santa Anita campaign with an effortless victory over her stablemate Whirlabout in the Santa Margarita Handicap.

The action now shifted to Washington Park, Illinois, where Busher competed for another 5 events in a similar 6-week period. Four of these were handicaps – 2 open to colts – and 1 was a match. Busher (ridden by Bailey) began by giving Twosy a 10lb and a 4½-length beating in the 1-mile Cleopatra Handicap before, reunited with Longden, she gained one of her most memorable victories in the Arlington Handicap (for three-year-olds and above) over 1¼ miles. Hot favourites to lift the $36,900 purse, the duo left nothing to chance and made all the running to win by 4 lengths with something in hand.

In the wake of this display the Beverley Handicap, confined to fillies, a fortnight later seemed a mere formality. Sensationally, Busher failed to concede 12lb and 26lb to the four-year-olds Duranza and Letmenow, tall order though this was since the younger horse would normally expect to receive not concede weight.

Mayer's pride had been dented and he considered Busher's honour at stake. A match at level weights was hastily arranged for August 29th with a purse of $25,000 going to the winner. This time there was no mistake, Busher winning by ¾ length. Now all that remained was to see how much this additional exertion had affected the filly's chances of collecting the meeting's major prize, the 1¼-mile Washington Park Handicap to be contested only 4 days after the match. Although Duranza was again in the field, the threat to Busher was rated to come from Pot o'Luck, a three-year-old colt who had run second in the Kentucky Derby and won the $67,000 Classic Stakes earlier at the meeting, and the four-year-old gelding Armed.

Busher winning the Washington Park Handicap

Once again, taking into account her age and sex, Busher was conceding weight all round. Not that it made the slightest bit of difference, for Longden brought her under the wire in a time of 2 minutes 1.8 seconds to break the thirteen-year-old track record. Duranza had set the tempo required for a record run, rapid even-paced quarters of 23.2, 23.4 and 24.0 before Armed relieved her of the chore.

Longden was biding his time, keeping his filly composed, talking her through the surge to come. "You use your voice in talking to a horse, to encourage or quiet her down but your most important communication comes through your hands. Just a delicate touch is enough – the motion of one finger or a slight turn of the wrist will tell the animal what you want." With barely 100 yards to go Longden gave Busher a "turn of the wrist" and she left the gelding, soon to win the Washington Handicap and the Pimlico Special, for dead.

Busher then shipped west for the Hollywood Park season on the other side of the continent. Possibly the enervating journey sapped a little of her energy for she lost by a head to Quick Reward (received 11lb) in her first engagement, the Will Rogers Handicap.

However, the Hollywood Derby and Vanity Handicap went more or less according to plan. The former registered her biggest purse of the year at $40,470 but more importantly included a handsome victory over Bymeabond which settled another old score. Breaking quickly from an outside draw Busher was bumped rounding the first turn but, immediately recovering her position, took command in the stretch to beat Man o'Glory cosily by 1½ lengths. Arguably this was the partnership's finest hour. Busher had given weight to all the others and produced the fastest time over the distance during the 35-day meeting, despite cruising the final furlong in a leisurely 13 seconds.

After securing her 10th victory of 1945 (and the 15th of her career), 8 of which came in stakes races, Busher's all-time earnings (including place money) rose to $334,035, placing her 7th in the world list behind Whirlaway and top of the fillies' table. Unfortunately she could not increase this total. During the last close season both her front ankles had been pinfired and on October 16th one gave way as she was being prepared for the Hollywood Gold Cup.

The active season may have ended for Busher and Longden yet much awaited them elsewhere. In the Daily Racing Form Awards announced on December 8th, Busher swept the poll. All 30 votes for the Horse of the Year were cast in her favour, an honour unprecedented in the 10-year history of the awards. Only 3 other females, before or since, have ever won the title. In addition she became the first filly since Top Flight in 1931 to head

Busher and John Longden, with Mayer (on right) after the Santa Susana Stakes at Santa Anita

the list of seasonal earnings with $273,735, a sum only surpassed previously by Gallant Fox in his Triple Crown winning season of 1930. For his part Longden finished the season with 180 winners worth nearly a million dollars in stakes – another new record – whilst Mayer and Odom came second and third in their respective categories.

The injury to Busher's leg proved worse than initially diagnosed and she missed the whole of the 1946 season. When she finally reappeared on January 2nd 1947 at Santa Anita, fully 15 months after her setback, it was obvious the old fire had been extinguished, as she trailed in fifth of 6. Busher never ran again and did not remain the property of Mayer for much longer. Twelve days after her defeat he announced his withdrawal from racing and his entire stock of 60 animals was auctioned on February 27th. Busher fell to a bid of $135,000 from Neil S McCarthy. Sentiment is a strong emotion. Within a year Mayer had bought her back and she ultimately threw a good winner in Jet Action who emulated his mother by winning the Washington Park Handicap of 1955 partnered by Willie Shoemaker.

Longden, meanwhile, went through the remainder of the 1940s on the crest of a wave, becoming champion again in 1947 and 1948, and racking up 2,012 wins during the decade. When he retired on March 12th 1966 after winning the San Juan Capistrano Handicap on George Royal, his 6,032nd winner (he passed Gordon Richards' world record on September 3rd 1956), he took to training and became the only man to both ride and train a Kentucky Derby winner when Majestic Prince won the 1969 "Run for the Roses".

Looking back over the great years and legendary horses he partnered only one filly stood out in his mind. "Busher was in a class by herself. I've handled a lot of good fillies but I doubt they could have beaten Busher doing anything. She had the heart of a lion, dead game, never gave up." Pausing a while, he would add a final, telling accolade. "Like all truly good ones she loved to run."

BUSHER

Chestnut filly 1942
Ran 21   Won 15   Placed 4   Value of Races Won $313,855

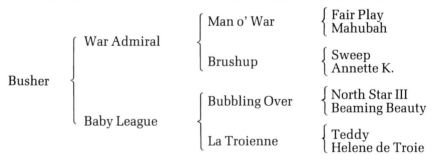

SEVEN

Petite Etoile and Lester Piggott

Wherever Lester Piggott fits into the gallery of great jockeys the assertion that he was a genius whose talents encompassed the entire spectrum of horsemanship is beyond question. From the 11 machine-gun strokes of his whip during the last furlong of the 1972 Derby which won the race for Roberto to that combination of tenderness and ice-cool resolve which nursed the temperamental and tiring Ribero to victory in the 1968 St Leger, the racing public has been treated to a veritable cornucopia of skills.

That Piggott was a mercurial character is also unquestioned – he could, and did, ride the occasional stinker – but when he partnered a grey filly by Petition out of Star of Iran in Manchester's Prestwich Stakes on May 30th 1958 he encountered a maverick spirit compatible with his own. "Petite Etoile was an awful monkey," according to her trainer Noel Murless, an affectionate view that could equally have applied to her jockey. Together Piggott and the "Little Star" lit up the racing firmament over 4 seasons.

Lester Piggott and Petite Etoile were positively made for each other. Both were immaculately bred for their respective jobs. Petite Etoile's sire had won an Eclipse and her dam was a full sister to the Arc winner Migoli and a great-granddaughter of Mumtaz Mahal, the "flying filly". This female line had already become synonymous with speed, for Mumtaz Mahal who won 7 of her 10 races including the Queen Mary, Nunthorpe and King George, and was a daughter of The Tetrarch the unbeaten two-year-old champion of 1913 and regarded as one of the Turf's fastest ever animals. Furthermore Petite Etoile was inbred to Lady Josephine (the dam of Mumtaz Mahal and grandam of Petition's sire Fair Trial), another notable influence for blinding speed.

Most of the Mumtaz Mahal family could also be counted upon for pyrotechnics, a trait forever linked with grey sprinters as a result. Petite Etoile's behaviour would prove no exception. On more than one occasion she got loose before a race, most notably on her debut and prior to the 1961 Victor Wild Stakes at Kempton. Murless remarked:

> "She was a peculiar animal. She was a grey and she loved having a grey in front of her in the string and more particularly a grey behind her when she went out to exercise. In my experience this was unique but then Petite Etoile was unique in every way. She was always on the go. She was like quicksilver under you."

How she hated strangers. One day her owner's stud manager Cyril Hall made a visit to Warren Place and viewed Petite Etoile in her box. "You're getting a bit fat old girl," he said prodding a finger into her neck. In a flash, the mare turned on him and picked him up by the coat lapels!

And yet Petite Etoile could be as meek as the baby in a Pears Soap advertisement. She returned to the winner's enclosure after the Yorkshire Oaks with blood pouring from a damaged tooth. Standing motionless, she allowed Murless to extract the offending molar and then quietly took a crop of grass. Her owner Prince Aly Khan, looking on in wonderment, was left to say, "You can breed for years and years and never get a filly as good as this one. I do not think we have bred one as good as this and I'm sure that I have never seen one as good." On the subject of his sweetheart Murless was unashamedly effusive.

> "Hers is a woman's face and a woman's character. She has a very nice, well-bred nature but if anything upsets her, well then, all hell breaks loose. She knows she's good. She doesn't stand for any other horses eating near her – she insists that they stay at a respectful distance. She is the most intelligent of animals I have ever known. She misses nothing. She instantly recognises me a hundred yards away and demands her present of sugar. She also has a wonderful sense of humour. Sometimes in the box I will pick up a stick and raise it to her in fun and she immediately picks up her leg at me!"

Many of the aforementioned sentiments and characteristics find an echo in the life of Lester Piggott. His own pedigree combined a male line running back through the jump jockey Piggotts and Tom Cannon, winner of 12 classics, to the Days of Danebury. Cannon's daughter Margaret married Ernie Piggott, rider of National winner Poethlyn, and their son Keith rode 500 winners over jumps before training Ayala to win the 1963 National. When Iris Rickaby married Keith in 1929 she contributed more racing blood. Father Fred had won 3 classics – all on fillies – while brother Fred's 5 classics were likewise gained on females, one of them Diadem. Moreover great-grandfather Rickaby trained the 1855 Derby winner Wild Dayrell.

It seemed the Rickabys had a way with fillies, a talent which Lester had obviously inherited. Brushes with senior jockeys and stewards he may have had but his delicate handling of Carrozza to win the 1957 Oaks and of the great Irish mare Gladness throughout 1958 testified to his uncanny flair with the fairer sex. The arrival of Petite Etoile would see this gift utilised to the full. "I think of all the rides I have seen Lester have," says former jockey Jimmy Lindley, "the way he used to ride Petite Etoile was the most impressive. She was not a true stayer but Lester seemed to be able to perform magic with her."

However, even the greatest genius would be taxed by Petite Etoile. Piggott is on record as saying:

> "She was always great fun to ride. She was intelligent and a goodlooker. Fillies as we all know can be deceptive. You sometimes find one who doesn't look all that much but will run until she drops. Petite Etoile did not really stay but she had this incredible burst of speed."

Harnessing this tremendous kick was never easy and therein lay the germ of unpredictability that typified the Piggott-Petite Etoile partnership.

The relationship started inauspiciously. Petite Etoile only came to Warren Place because Aly Khan's French trainer Alec Head declined to take her

Petite Etoile and
Lester Piggott

and even the Murless yard was chock-full of female talent in 1958 in the shape of Collyria, Rose of Medina, Short Sentence and Parrotia. Choosing a classic partner for 1959 would be no simple matter for the stable jockey but, superficially at least, appeared somewhat easier after Petite Etoile's debut at Manchester. Petite Etoile's allegedly sprinting pedigree was one thing but her antics this day surely ruled out any prospects of classic glory. The afternoon was cold and wet, no conditions for a prima donna, which is just what Petite Etoile decided to impersonate. First she reared up on the way from the stables to the paddock, knocking out her lad, got loose again in the paddock itself and then, in no fit state to do herself justice, was beaten 8 lengths by her solitary opponent, Chris. Admittedly Chris was a useful horse who had already won 3 times and would eventually number a victory in the Kings' Stand to his credit but this really was a shambles. If all this was not bad enough the filly twice got loose after the race and galloped backwards and forwards a considerable time before being recaptured.

Murless prescribed a 6-week break in an effort to overcome an experience which would have fascinated any equine psychiatrist. The treatment succeeded for Petite Etoile showed no signs of fright at Sandown on July 12th when defeating Miss Romper by 5 lengths in the Star Stakes. She could not handle Krakenwake in Goodwood's Molecomb Stakes at the end of the month (beaten 2 lengths after a slow start) but in her final outing on August 13th, the Rose Stakes at Sandown, she once more won comfortably. Both her victories had been over 5 furlongs and despite receiving 8 stone 6lb in the Free Handicap (10lb behind the leading fillies Lindsay and Rosalba), the chances of her lasting the Guineas mile, let alone the $1\frac{1}{2}$ miles of the Oaks, appeared remote.

Such was the supposed strength of the Warren Place three-year-old fillies in the spring of 1959 that Lester Piggott twice rejected Petite Etoile in favour of others. Murless decided to run Petite Etoile in the Free Handicap over 7 furlongs of the Guineas course in order to gauge her stamina. As the weights rose 8lb she carried 9 stone top weight which included Aly Khan's French-based Australian jockey George Moore, since it had been thought prudent for Piggott to partner the Queen's Short Sentence. Always travelling well, Petite Etoile took the lead in the dip to win smoothly by 3 lengths.

No fewer than 4 other Murless fillies joined Petite Etoile in the paddock before the 1,000 Guineas making Piggott's choice all the more arduous. He elected to remain loyal to Collyria even though she was making her seasonal debut. Doug Smith had ridden Petite Etoile in her final workout, and knowing how impressive she had been (Clive Brittain, then working for Murless, has related how Piggott was fed doubtful information by one lad in order to settle an old score), readily accepted the mount and enjoyed an effortless 1-length victory over Rosalba, with Collyria back in fifth. The time was 2 seconds faster than that of Taboun in the previous day's 2,000 Guineas.

The cat was now well and truly out of the bag and although Petite Etoile did not run again before the Oaks and her stamina had to be taken on trust, Piggott had no intention of partnering Collyria (or Rose of Medina) on this occasion. The principal threat lay with the northern filly Cantelo who started favourite on the basis of a 6-length success in the Cheshire Oaks in a very fast time. However, despite a ferocious pace (only 2 Oaks have been run faster) Cantelo had failed to lose Petite Etoile as they rounded Tattenham Corner. Piggott positioned the grey right on Cantelo's tail and there he lurked until well below the distance. Then, in a trice, she was off and 3 lengths clear at the post. The stopwatch repeated the lesson of the Guineas for the colts had been 0.2 seconds slower in the Derby.

The filly won her first 3 victories of 1959 by an aggregate of 7 lengths; she would win the next 3 by a mere 2 lengths as a result of this mixture of Piggott cheekiness and her cat-like ability to accelerate. In the Sussex Stakes over a mile she strolled to a $\frac{3}{4}$-length win over Piping Rock and in the Yorkshire Oaks experienced no difficulty (apart perhaps from the troublesome tooth) in beating Mirnaya by a similar margin. The latter success raised her winnings to £46,235, an all-time record for an English filly.

Piggott's avowed belief in Petite Etoile's ability to "paralyse anything in a burst of 100 yards – which can make both horse and jockey look the best in the world", very nearly caused the duo to come unstuck in their final outing of the season, the $1\frac{1}{4}$ mile Champion Stakes.

It has been written that by this point Murless and Hall were becoming perceptibly edgy at Piggott's regular tight-rope act on Petite Etoile. "Lester, let us go easy on anxiety today please," the trainer is reported to have said as his jockey mounted the grey filly. No words could have more assuredly invited exactly the opposite. Petite Etoile only faced two rivals, the Irish St Leger winner Barclay and the Eclipse runner-up Javelot, yet somehow she and Piggott engineered a scenario where they were shut-in with less than a furlong to go. The 3 runners dawdled through the first half of the race and the riders of Barclay and Javelot were not now about to open a gap through which Piggott could unleash Petite Etoile's devastating speed. Seconds ticked away and Piggott switched the filly to the rails where only the narrowest chink of daylight existed between Javelot and the fence. It appeared for all the world that Freddie Palmer on Javelot would seal the gap, as he was entitled to do, necessitating the sprouting of wings if the filly was to win. Fortunately, either through Palmer's chivalry or Javelot veering under pressure, a tiny opening remained through which Petite Etoile could be launched. The judge's verdict was $\frac{1}{2}$ length; the medication prescribed to Messrs Hall and Murless is unrecorded, as were their words to Piggott who confined himself to the dry comment, "I could still have run round the other side and won."

Since her Oaks' victim Cantelo had beaten the colts in the St Leger, the status of Petite Etoile as the premier three-year-old was undisputed, the official handicapper assessing her 5lb superior to the Derby winner Parthia and 2lb superior to the Arc winner St Crespin. Unofficially some were talking of Petite Etoile as the best filly since the "peerless" Pretty Polly, winner of 22 races between 1903–06 including the 1,000 Guineas, Oaks, St Leger, Champion Stakes and two Coronation Cups, in several of which she humbled the Derby winner of her generation. Petite Etoile was given the opportunity to emulate Pretty Polly because she stayed in training with the intention of meeting Parthia in both the 1960 Coronation Cup and King George & Queen Elizabeth Stakes.

Pretty Polly and Petite Etoile shared a special penchant for winning by little more than was necessary. Consequently, as with her illustrious forerunner, the inevitable question was posed concerning the amount she actually had in reserve at the conclusion of these nerve-jangling contests. Were Piggott's exaggerated waiting tactics masking the true extent of her greatness or concealing an inherent lack of stamina that could be exposed in a fast-run $1\frac{1}{2}$ mile race? In the Coronation Cup Cecil Boyd-Rochfort determined to find out and ran the Queen's good colt Above Suspicion as a pacemaker for Parthia.

The ploy failed. After a bloodless victory in Kempton's Victor Wild Stakes on May 7th the filly came to Epsom a month later and positively toyed with the 2 colts who constituted her only opposition. In spite of the Derby winner's presence Petite Etoile started 3/1 on favourite. Piggott sat behind the Boyd-Rochfort pair until a furlong out where a slight twitch of the reins sent the grey filly $1\frac{1}{2}$ lengths clear in a matter of moments. The time of 2 minutes 35.2 seconds was 0.6 seconds faster than the previous day's Derby and emphasized the race had been a true test. As a mark of respect for Aly Khan, tragically killed in a car crash 2 weeks earlier, no one led the filly into the winner's circle.

Everything seemed on course for a triumphal reprise over the best Europe could muster in Ascot's King George & Queen Elizabeth Stakes on July 16th. Murless wanted to give her one more race in between – Newmarket's Princess of Wales's Stakes – but on the morning of the race she coughed, and though her temperature was normal, she was scratched. A week before Ascot she worked well over a mile and she certainly lost no marks in appearance when

Petite Etoile winning the Oaks

the King George field circled the paddock. On the debit side, the going was soft and among her opponents were runners committed to a fast pace from the outset.

De Voos set the early gallop ahead of Parthia, with Petite Etoile in rear. However once into the short Ascot straight Aggressor, a gutsy stayer, set sail for the winning post. By the time Piggott and Petite Etoile had extricated themselves from behing a wall of horses (giving Kythnos a hefty bump in the process) Aggressor had stolen a priceless advantage. Initially Piggott still oozed confidence but as soon as the customary acceleration failed to materialize, he began to ride the filly in earnest. Some believed Petite Etoile almost reached the colt 150 yards out. Whatever the case, Aggressor had a $\frac{1}{2}$-length advantage when they passed the post. Piggott said afterwards:

> "I should have won. I took what I thought was the best way on the outside because there was a wall of horses in front of the filly and Aggressor. At that moment the horses in front of us split up and Jimmy Lindley on Aggressor was able to go through on the inside. I had to go a little before time and, with Aggressor away, Petite Etoile could not produce her speed for long enough. We were dead before we got near the post."

The partnership's much-touted invincibility had been rudely shattered.

Explanations abounded. The ground, softer than she had encountered hitherto; the strong gallop; the bump with Kythnos cost her valuable impetus; the after-effects of the cough. Years later Scobie Breasley even confessed to deliberately hindering the filly's progress as a means of repaying Piggott for having done the same to him earlier in the year. The cruellest barb, however, suggested that Piggott had given her far too much leeway to make up. Perhaps the order had been a tall one yet she had her chance with $1\frac{1}{2}$ furlongs remaining, as she had on numerous other occasions, and could not capitalize upon it this time of asking. Murless must have got nearer to the truth when he said, "She never really got more than $1\frac{1}{4}$ miles and we knew that if anyone took her on from start to finish in a $1\frac{1}{2}$ mile race that she would not stay. A lot of people blamed Lester but I never did."

Although Piggott and Petite Etoile raced 6 more times, the magic associated with their partnership evaporated after Ascot and they tasted defeat twice more. These 2 reverses came in the 1961 season since Petite Etoile did indeed succumb to the cough before her next intended appearance in the Queen Elizabeth II Stakes. Her final campaign opened much as usual with 3 victories by a head, neck and 1 length in the Coronation Stakes, Coronation Cup and Rous Memorial Stakes respectively. Nonetheless, in the first 2 races some judges were convinced she could not have beaten Wordpam and Vienna by precious more. She'd sweated and showed reluctance to line-up at Epsom. If all this was true Petite Etoile was deteriorating. Sadly the knockers were proved correct when she failed to peg back High Hat in Kempton's Aly Khan International Memorial Gold Cup, a race her young owner the Aga Khan would have loved her to win above all others. High Hat set a scorching pace virtually the whole way and the Aga saw the mare's tail swish testily as Piggott unavailingly tried to reduce the 2-length deficit entering the straight. "He ran me into the ground," said Piggott by way of explanation rather than excuse.

Victory at Kempton would have ensured immediate retirement. "A five-year-old mare is not an easy proposition," admitted Murless. "She had done marvellously well to keep going as long as that. You've got to string mares up if you are going to keep them on and if they are going to take on the colts. I think it is against the run of nature, although in the case of Petite Etoile she didn't need a lot of work." However it was felt she ought to be given the opportunity of redeeming herself and the new Aga had little else with which to stimulate his interest in the Turf. A revised programme was mapped-out for the rest of the season. Such plans were promptly thwarted when she picked up a thorn, resulting in a bruised heel, and it was 2 months before she was seen again. Doncaster's 1-mile Scarborough Stakes proved the partnership's swansong. Petite Etoile looked on her toes and beat Fulshaw Cross without undue stress, but a fortnight ater the duo were forced to give best to Le Levanstell in the Queen Elizabeth II Stakes, a result which showed quite emphatically that the mare was but a shadow of her former self.

"A super horse is like a super human being. It has to have the physical capabilities and then it has to have that something extra. It has to have that will to win." Noel Murless's words applied to both his favourite filly and her jockey. Piggott went on to accumulate a record 29 classic victories and 11 jockeys' championships, becoming mellower by the year. Petite Etoile, on the other hand, proved mercurial to the end. Like many a great race mare she was disappointing at stud. Of her 3 foals to survive only Afaridaan managed to win, and that only a small race in France.

PETITE ETOILE

Grey filly 1956
Ran 19   Won 14   Placed 5   Value of Races Won £67,785

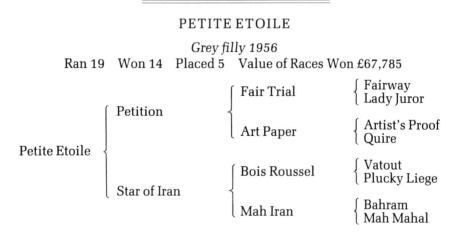

		Fair Trial	Fairway / Lady Juror
	Petition		
		Art Paper	Artist's Proof / Quire
Petite Etoile			
		Bois Roussel	Vatout / Plucky Liege
	Star of Iran		
		Mah Iran	Bahram / Mah Mahal

EIGHT

Noblesse and Garnie Bougoure

Anyone unfamiliar with the British racing scene of the early 1960s who happened to catch a glimpse of Garnie Bougoure could be excused the conclusion that the Australian jockey's trouble-worn countenance betrayed a career singularly devoid of success. Though not quite in the class of Lester Piggott's "well-kept grave", Bougoure's face exhibited a gaunt expression which in many walks of life would be indicative of a miserable existence. Yet nothing could be further from the truth in Bougoure's case. After a period as first jockey to the O'Brien stable, yielding Irish classic victories on Light Year (1961 2,000 Guineas), Chamour (1960 Derby) and Barclay (1959 St Leger), Bougoure followed his compatriot Ron Hutchinson as stable jockey to Paddy Prendergast, an appointment which saw him strike up partnerships with some of the greatest Irish horses of the decade. Flying two-year-olds such as Whistling Wind and middle-distance stars like Ragusa and Khalkis all benefited from the quiet Bougoure touch. In 1963–4 the Prendergast-Bougoure combination won 5 classics in England and Ireland. Four of these came in a glorious 1963 when they won the Irish Derby and St Leger (Prendergast horses also won both Guineas without Bougoure) and the English Oaks and St Leger, in addition to the Eclipse, King George & Queen Elizabeth and a host of other top races. Prendergast's total winnings of £202,894 from 46 races established a new training record.

The English Oaks triumph of that *annus mirabilis* was something special. It was the first by an Irish filly and she equalled Formosa's record 10-length margin of victory in so doing. Her name was Noblesse and many, Bougoure included, regarded her as the best of all the Prendergast stars. "I've been riding a long time," said the normally reserved Bougoure, "but this is definitely the greatest horse I have ever been on".

Bougoure's inscrutable features were perfectly matched by the enigmatic nature of Noblesse's career. She was beset by numerous niggling injuries and only ran 5 times in 2 seasons. Her 4 victories in the Blue Seal Stakes,

Timeform Gold Cup, Musidora Stakes and the Oaks hardly caused Bougoure to stir her from a canter yet she won them by an aggregate of 24 lengths. If her opponents were mediocre she could do no more than treat them with the contempt they deserved and this she surely did. Bougoure believed she could have won the Derby despite the presence of Relko and Ragusa, 2 exceptional animals in their own right, an opinion given credence by both the Jockey Club's official handicapper and Timeform at the end of the season. In the Free Handicap Relko, winner of the Derby, French 2,000 Guineas and St Leger, headed the weights on 9st 7lb, 3lb ahead of Noblesse which suggested he could not have beaten her at Epsom, where he would have conceded 5lb. Ragusa, who had won the Irish Derby, King George and St Leger, was on 9st 6lb and thus rated slightly inferior to his female stable companion after the sex allowance was deducted. One pound behind Noblesse came the brilliant grey French filly Hula Dancer, winner of the 1,000 Guineas and Champion Stakes. In comparison Timeform rated the quartet Ragusa 137, Relko 136 and the 2 fillies equal on 133.

In what constituted, therefore, a vintage crop of three-year-olds a case could be made for saying that Noblesse was the best. In truth there was no telling how good she was for after suffering her first defeat, in the Prix Vermeille, she was found to be irrevocably lame and retired without ever having experienced the acid test for all classic fillies, namely confrontation with the classic colts of her generation.

Noblesse's delicate appearance – she was rather a small, sparely-made chestnut who only impressed when she was galloping – belied her early foaling date of January 24th. She was bred by the Canadian Mrs P. G. Margetts and born at Lt-Col Douglas Gray's Hadrian Stud in Newmarket where her dam Duke's Delight, having been covered again by Mossborough at the New England Stud, was being boarded prior to leaving for North America. Noblesse's pedigree did not seem to be out of the top drawer. Mossborough had not been top class himself. All told he ran 17 times for 5 wins, his best performance probably being his second place to Mystery IX in the 1951 Eclipse. At stud he proved more successful, leading the list in 1958 thanks to the exploits of Ballymoss. However, although Anticlea had won him the Italian 1,000 Guineas and Oaks, Mossborough had sired nothing else in this class until Noblesse came along.

The distaff side of Noblesse's pedigree was even more unprepossessing. Duke's Delight (by 1937 Coronation Cup winner His Grace, a full brother to Derby winner Blenheim) managed to win 3 small races back in the 1940s and had produced 5 winners from her previous 8 foals, none of whom were outstanding. In fact the best of Noblesse's close relatives was her contemporary Irish Chorus (out of Duke's Delight's daughter Dawn Chorus) who won

5 races in 1962 and was considered the fastest juvenile in Ireland until Noblesse appeared later in the season. Neither of the next 2 dams, Early Light and Sun Mist, won a race though they each bred a few winners. One had to go back 7 generations to Sterling Balm, the grandam of St Louis (1922 2,000 Guineas) and Silver Urn (1922 1,000 Guineas) and the fourth dam of Silversol (1936 Irish Oaks) and Sol Oriens (1941 Irish Derby) to discover a female influence of any consequence. By a strange twist of fate the family fortunes took a turn for the better in the 1960s for besides the fame brought by Noblesse, her niece Irish Chorus bred Saritamer, winner of the Cork & Orrery, July Cup and Diadem Stakes who in turn sired Time Charter, and a sister of Irish Chorus named George's Girl produced the French Oaks winner Pistol Packer.

By some miracle or other, as it seemed at the time (the role of Mossborough's sire Nearco should not be underestimated), a racehorse of exceptional talent emerged from this somewhat plebean mixture of bloodlines. Indeed, the Hadrian Stud took the trouble to insert a half-page advertisement for their "quality filly" in the 1961 Sales Issue of the British Racehorse in an effort to stimulate interest. Whatever its impact, Noblesse fell to a bid of 4,200 guineas from the Anglo-Irish Agency on behalf of the American Mrs J. M. Olin, a patron of the Prendergast stable.

P. J. "Darkie" Prendergast, whose relatively unsuccessful career as a steeplechase jockey had been terminated by a broken neck, took out a trainer's licence in 1943 and embarked on a new career of practically continuous success. He started with just 1 horse, Pelorus, which promptly won 7 races but his amazing ability to spot potential flying machines saw him graduate to greater things at Ascot, Goodwood and York courtesy of The Pie King, Windy City, Paddy's Sister, Floribunda and La Tendresse. Between 1950 and 1965 a Prendergast-trained two-year-old topped the Irish Free Handicap on no less than 12 occasions. His first classic arrived in 1950 when the appropriately-named Dark Warrior won the Irish Derby. By the time of his death on Ascot Gold Cup day 1980 Prendergast had trained the winners of 21 Irish and English classics and become, in 1963, the first Irish-based trainer to lead the English table, an achievement he repeated for the next 2 seasons.

Prendergast held Australian jockeyship in the highest esteem and in 1960 invited Ron Hutchinson to Rossmore Lodge as his jockey. Together they won that year's English 2,000 Guineas with Martial and the Irish version with Kythnos before Hutchinson moved across the Irish Sea to take up a post with the Duke of Norfolk's private stable in 1962.

Hutchinson's well-nourished appearance was made to look positively plump by the wizened, leathery features of Garnet "Garnie" Bougoure.

Battling the scales in the hot climates of Australia and the Far East made Bougoure seem at least 10 years older than his actual age of 36. However British racegoers had received plentiful evidence from Scobie Breasley that weather-beaten Australians were to be respected where it mattered – out on the track. Based in Melbourne, Bougoure had ridden largely for Flemington trainer Theo Lewis and was equally effective in short races as long ones, having won such diverse events as the Doomben Cup, Doncaster Handicap and the Brisbane Cup. Like his friend Breasley, who had recommended him to Prendergast, he learned to ride against the clock and was a superb judge of pace as a result. He also shared some of Breasley's infinite horsemanship. Bougoure seldom hit a horse, preferring to use his whip as a means of maintaining his mount's balance and rhythm. Skills like these made Bougoure invaluable on the Prendergast two-year-olds or any filly who needed careful handling. Thus he was in the right place at the right time to become the ideal partner for Noblesse.

The 1962 season was drawing to a close when Noblesse made her debut

Noblesse and Garnie Bourgoure

in Ascot's Blue Seal Stakes over 6 furlongs on September 29th. Slow to come to hand, she had been turned out of training at the beginning of April and did not return until June. Not for the first time the sunshine of summer worked its wizardry on the female of the species. Noblesse was galloped with Display, beaten just $\frac{1}{2}$ length in the 1,000 Guineas, and she pulverised the older filly by 4 lengths. Bougoure and Prendergast could not believe their eyes and were convinced Display must have gone wrong, but a week afterwards she won the Coronation Stakes at Royal Ascot. When the pair were worked a second time together Noblesse won by 12 lengths. To say that Rossmore Lodge, never afraid of a little punt, wore its betting boots on the day of the Blue Seal would be a wild understatement. "We knew we had something to go to war with," is how Paddy Prendergast junior described it.

However, a "whisper" such as this proved impossible to conceal. Noblesse opened up a 2/1 favourite to beat her 20 opponents but as the money poured in, she shortened to 11/8 by the off with 10/1 the next best in the market. "The breeze from Ireland about Noblesse proved a reliable trade wind," *The Sporting Life* cryptically observed in the wake of Noblesse's scintillating 5-length victory. Drawn on the outside, Bougoure chose to bring the filly quietly up the far rail. By halfway she had pulled herself past Dinant and Philippa's Choice and effectively settled the outcome in a matter of strides. Eased 20 yards out, Noblesse passed the post back on the bridle, scarcely realizing she had been in a race. Nevertheless, the clock stated that she had covered the 6 furlongs in a time 0.43 seconds faster than the smart three-year-old sprinter Compensation in the previous race.

As the Cheveley Park Stakes, the traditional end-of-season target for juvenile fillies, was to be run only 4 days later. Prendergast had to search elsewhere if Noblesse were to be given another run. With opportunities dwindling he decided to throw her in at the deep end against the colts in the Timeform Gold Cup at Doncaster on October 20th. Run over a mile, the race was in its second year having been instituted by the Halifax organization as an authentic test for future classic horses along the lines of France's Grand Criterium. The inaugural winner Miralgo had disappointed in the Derby but finished second in the St Leger. A first prize of £23,338, more than 4 times the second richest two-year-old event, guaranteed the participation of most holding classic pretensions.

Once again Noblesse was a warm order, at 11/10. Prendergast had recently galloped her with Featheredge, beaten a neck in the Diadem Stakes, and Noblesse slaughtered the three-year-old. The dangers, on paper at any rate, were Star Moss, a 3-length winner of the 1 mile Royal Lodge Stakes at Ascot the day before the Blue Seal, Partholon winner of The Curragh's

National Stakes (by a neck from Prendergast's Molino – so that formline was known) and Portofino, who had won his only race at Newmarket.

The 50/1 shot Nearall cut out the early running. Turning into the long Doncaster straight Star Moss and Partholon went on, with at this point Bougoure and Noblesse lobbing along some 4 lengths behind the leaders, exuding an air of utter indifference. However upon the merest encouragement from Bougoure the filly lengthened her stride and, rapidly overhauling the 2 colts, opened a gap of 5 lengths. No sooner had Bougoure unleashed Noblesse than it appeared he had her back on the bridle again. She cruised the final 150 yards yet equalled the two-year-old track record of 1 minute 38.4 seconds. "Noblesse is the queen of them all after a breathtaking win," is how the *Life* summarized her afternoon's exercise.

Not surprisingly in view of her 2 imperious displays Noblesse was the top-rated filly in the Free Handicap on 9st 4lb, just the 3lb sex allowance below the Middle Park winner Crocket, and throughout the winter her clash with the unbeaten Hula Dancer in the 1,000 Guineas was eagerly anticipated.

Unfortunately Noblesse and the spring were again incompatible. Taking on a filly of Hula Dancer's class at half-cock would have been suicidal and Prendergast had little alternative but to scratch Noblesse early in April. Further work on the Monday after the Guineas (Hula Dancer having duly won) failed to impress either and she left the Irish equivalent to her stablemate Gazpacho who won by $2\frac{1}{2}$ lengths on a tight rein. On a line through Hera, Gazpacho would have troubled Hula Dancer at Newmarket. What kind of filly did that make Noblesse?

Prendergast got her ready to run for York's Musidora Stakes over an extended $1\frac{1}{4}$ miles on May 15th, although she did not please paddock commentators. She had grown very little and still lacked her summer coat. Market opposition was so strong that she started at even money after opening at odds-on. What the odds-layers were not cogniscent of this day were details of Noblesse's latest piece of work over $4\frac{1}{2}$ furlongs with the sprinter Polybius. Bougoure was ordered to "shake up" Noblesse if she ran lazily. Accordingly, halfway through the gallop, he pulled his whip through and instantaneously the filly bolted 4 lengths clear! "I thought Polybius must have broken down," he explained to attentive reporters after the Musidora. Armed with this knowledge 30 minutes earlier there would doubtless have been several journalists noticeably better off.

The Musidora field was by no means mediocre but Noblesse made them look platers just the same. Royal Agreement, making the pace for Noblesse, brought them into the straight whereupon Crenelle, a promising third on her debut and receiving 10lb from Noblesse, struck the front. What followed seemed a carbon-copy of the Timeform Gold Cup. Bougoure slipped Noblesse out of the pack and still on a tight rein drew up to Crenelle and swallowed her in a few seconds. Sprinting away she won by 6 lengths from Olgiata (winner of the Wood Ditton by 4 lengths on her debut), which could have been doubled had Bougoure moved a muscle. Anyone attempting to decry the quality of this performance on the grounds of inferior opposition again found the stopwatch providing irrefutable evidence to the contrary. Noblesse had covered the distance 1.2 seconds faster than the classic colts in the Dante Stakes.

The result of the Musidora insisted that the Oaks was a foregone conclusion for Noblesse since Hula Dancer could not stay the distance and was a non-runner. The 8 fillies ranged against Noblesse could not be described as high-class in comparison and she was the shortest-priced favourite since the war at 11/4 on. But the way she destroyed them had to be seen to be believed. Tales of her "wonder filly" enticed Mrs Evelyn Olin from the United States and she must have regretted not coming earlier by the end of the afternoon. Held up at the rear of the field, Noblesse advanced to sixth place rounding Tattenham Corner, effortlessly progressed to challenge Spree a furlong out, dashed past her and was back on the bit passing the

Noblesse winning the Oaks

post with Bougoure looking over his left shoulder for non-existent challengers.

To discover any danger Bougoure would have needed binoculars for Spree was 10 lengths in arrears. "This was the most overwhelming classic victory I have ever seen," said the experienced and respected Tom Nickalls of *The Sporting Life.* Bougoure admitted the winning margin could have been doubled – "Just show her daylight and away she goes," – while Jimmy Lindley, rider of the second, epitomised the incredulity running through the crowd when he said, "Suddenly I heard a crack of hooves and Noblesse went by me like an express train. It was an absolute revelation." Prendergast now found himself with an embarrassment of riches. Khalkis won the Eclipse; Ragusa the Irish Derby. Finding suitably rich pickings for his trio of three-year-old stars would not be easy. Khalkis was to be aimed at the Great Voltigeur and then the Arc, Ragusa the Gordon Stakes and the Champion leaving the King George, Yorkshire Oaks and St Leger for Noblesse, with the proviso that if any mishap prevented Khalkis running at Longchamp Noblesse would deputise. In the event Khalkis was not seen out after Sandown due to a bout of acute enteritis which nearly killed him, Noblesse hit a hock and was scratched from the King George on July 12th, thereby allowing Ragusa to successfully replace her at Ascot and Doncaster and Khalkis at York. However there was just a chance Noblesse would contest the Arc if she came through the Prix Vermeille satisfactorily over the same course and distance in early September.

The injured hock cost Noblesse 2 or 3 weeks' preparation and as the field included the first 4 in the French Oaks her task was quite formidable. Nevertheless, in spite of not seeing a racecourse for almost 4 months she was made a 5/2 on favourite. It was estimated that at least £10,000 had been passed on to Tote agents by English bookmakers.

Coming down the Longchamp hill Noblesse was 6 lengths behind the leader Chutney, fourth in the French Oaks and twice a winner subsequently, who immediately quickened the pace upon gaining the straight. At the furlong pole Noblesse was in a challenging position but for the first time in her life she felt the sting of Bougoure's whip. The response was negative and Bougoure would not bring himself to set about her in earnest. They came fourth, half a dozen lengths behind the fast-finishing Golden Girl (only seventh in the French Oaks) who collared Chutney on the line. Clearly this was not the real Noblesse.

On returning to Ireland Noblesse was not only found to be sexually amiss but also lame. All thoughts of a retrieving operation in the Arc were promptly abandoned. Worse followed. After a thorough veterinary examination the damage was diagnosed as irreparable. On September 27th Noblesse was retired. She had won £46,444 from her 4 victories but left countless questions unanswered. That she was the best Irish-trained filly of all time is indisputable. Timeform considered her 1lb inferior to Petite Etoile and 2lb below Pebbles among postwar British middle-distance fillies with only Allez France, Dahlia, Coronation and All Along her superiors in Europe. Moreover anyone remembering the Oaks would be foolish to dismiss out of hand the possibility that in receipt of the 5lb she could not have defeated Relko on Derby day.

Noblesse crossed the Atlantic to start a new career which involved that same sense of what-might-have-been as its racing predecessor. She had 5 foals – all of whom proved winners – before tragically breaking a leg in 1972 and having to be put down. Where You Lead emulated her dam by winning the 1973 Musidora but could only finish second in the Oaks while Carezza was successful in the Nell Gwyn Stakes. More poignantly Where You Lead's daughter I Will Follow became the dam of Rainbow Quest who salvaged his great-grandam's honour by competing in, and winning, an Arc.

Garnie Bougoure stayed at Rossmore Lodge for another season. Then, after 2 more seasons riding in England mainly for Arthur Budgett, he packed his bags and headed back to sunnier climes, to train in Singapore, realizing that however long he trains he is unlikely to encounter another Noblesse.

NOBLESSE

Chestnut filly 1960
Ran 5   Won 4   Value of Races Won £46,443

		Nearco	Pharos
	Mossborough		Nogara
		All Moonshine	Bobsleigh
Noblesse			Selene
		His Grace	Blandford
	Duke's Delight		Malva
		Early Light	Easton
			Sun Mist

NINE

Allez France and Yves Saint-Martin

Allez France – the name has a ring to it that no Frenchman could possibly resist. Especially if it adorned a lady, a queen in fact, the Queen of Longchamp. Any queen deserves to be partnered by a king or at the very least by a prince. To the delight of French turfites in the 1970s their idol Allez France was ridden in every one of her 21 races by the "Little Prince" himself, the darling of the crowd, Yves Saint-Martin. Together they won 13 of them, 12 from 17 at Longchamp. It is therefore entirely appropriate that the onetime "wonder boy" of French racing should be eternally linked with the "wonder filly". A measure of their intertwined destinies came in 1974 when in order to partner Allez France in the Arc, arguably their finest hour, Saint-Martin had to be pumped with painkiller to mask the effects of an accident at Maisons-Laffitte. There was no way he would not ride. "I tell them it is OK because she is *my* filly, Allez France."

Regal though Allez France's track persona may have been she could be as tetchy as the Queen of Hearts back home at Chantilly. Her only confidante was an old sheep (in actual fact two old sheep since she killed the first one) and she could be evil toward any lady-in-waiting who tried to usurp her throne. On numerous occasions Allez France turned on her stablemate Lianga, a charming filly possessing impeccable manners and the speed to win a July Cup and the Prix de l'Abbaye. And although he acknowledged her enormous talent, trainer Angel Penna could never love Allez France as he did Lianga or his special sweetheart Pawneese, heroine of the 1976 Oaks, King George and Prix de Diane ("In the whole of France she was the best friend I ever made."). The Argentinian had an uncanny knack with fillies whom he treated like all other women. "Sometimes you can treat them badly and get away with it but the only certain way to make them lay down their lives for you is to love them." His voice always carried conviction when he insisted, "Believe me when I say Allez France at her best was the finest filly ever to run in Europe."

Whatever her disposition toward her fellowkind Allez France could certainly run, and run fast enough to beat the top colts, the true sign of a great race mare. Seven times out of 7 she defeated that other magnificent French filly Dahlia and her Timeform rating of 136 has not been surpassed by any elder female. Some commentators criticised her looks. She was too masculine – a jibe previously hurled at other great race mares like Pretty Polly in England and Busher in America. By an odd coincidence Allez France was related to Busher, both having descended from La Troienne who was the grandam of Busher and the fourth dam of Allez France. The 3 mares between La Troienne and Allez France were all high-class performers. Her dam Priceless Gem, the second best two-year-old of her year, won 7 races and was a sister to the stakes winner Admiring and a half-sister to Affectionately, winner of 28 races and the dam of Preakness winner Personality, American Horse of the Year in 1970. The second dam Searching showed similar class in the 1950s winning 25 races in 5 seasons and her dam Big Hurry (Black Toney and La Troienne), a full sister to Bimelech (Preakness and Belmont) and Black Helene (Coaching Club American Oaks, Florida Derby and American Derby) won 4 times and was a speedy sort. Thus Big Hurry was a half-sister to Baby League, the dam of Busher. This family also numbered the likes of Boucher and Buckpasser, American Horse of the Year in 1966, so that the French art dealer Daniel Wildenstein, intent on amassing representatives from all the world's most successful families, who had tried unsuccessfully to purchase Priceless Gem when she was sold for a record brood mare price of $395,000 in 1970, was determined to acquire her filly foal of that year by none other than France's own champion Sea Bird, widely acknowledged as the best thoroughbred to race there since the war and, with the possible exception of Ribot, the outstanding postwar animal in the whole of Europe. On this occasion Wildenstein got his horse, buying Priceless Gem's daughter privately from Hirsch Jacobs of Stymie Manor Farm, Kentucky for $160,000 and naming her Allez France.

Speed was the forte of Allez France's female line and everyone who saw Sea Bird's performances in the 1965 Derby or Arc (a 6-length victory from probably the strongest field ever assembled for the race) knew that he was not deficient in that department either. It was not long before Allez France provided dramatic evidence of her inheritance. Having won her debut race at Longchamp on September 1st 1972 she returned a month later on Arc Sunday to win the hotly-contested Criterium des Pouliches, also over a mile. Entering the straight Allez France had only one of her 15 rivals behind her and, furthermore, she was trapped on the rails. With 2 furlongs remaining she must have had 15 lengths to recover from virtually a standing start once Saint-Martin found an opening. The response from Allez France was breathtaking because she stormed up the straight to show the European racing community just what the future held. On breeding she possessed the stamina to complement this staggering acceleration and her two victories were gained on extremes of ground, soft and then firm. San San may have won the Arc 40 minutes earlier but Allez France was the name on most people's lips as the huge crowd dispersed and its thoughts turned to the classics of 1973.

Despite a career which had already brought 16 French classics and 3 English classics (figures which have subsequently risen to 29 and 7 respectively), no one savoured the new season's prospects more than Yves Saint-Martin. Born on September 8th 1941 at Agen, Saint-Martin overcame the wishes of his parents who never liked the idea of their son becoming a jockey. His first acquaintance with horses came at the prison camp for collaborators where his father worked at the end of the war. He befriended two huge carthorses and to everyone's astonishment would sit for hours talking to

Allez France and Yves Saint-Martin

them. Then, at the age of 5, he was taken to a local race meeting at Toulouse and his ambitions crystallised. With the help of family friends whose son was apprenticed to François Mathet's Chantilly stable, Saint-Martin took up his apprenticeship on September 15th, 1955, aged 14. "I was 32 kilos, I had no experience but I am very happy because I am going to work with horses." Within a year his parents' apprehension was fanned when he experienced a crashing fall on the exercise grounds which broke both wrists and left doctors convinced he would never ride again.

However Saint-Martin overcame any misgivings and in July 1958 made his debut on Good Lord at Soissons, an unfashionable course some 50 miles north-east of Paris, and 3 rides later, on July 26th, partnered Royallic to victory at Le Tremblay. By the end of the season Saint-Martin had ridden 21 winners and 2 years on, aged 19, he took the first of his 15 Jockeys' Championship with 107 wins. Although 3 months' National Service reduced Saint-Martin's 1961 total his career has not wavered since. In 1961 he won his first French classic on Solitude and a year afterwards his first in England. In 1964 he rode a French record of 184 winners, despite a 6-week suspension during a particularly lucrative run for the Mathet horses that would have taken him over the 200 mark.

The "Golden Boy" had become universally accepted as the finest French jockey of all by the advent of Allez France in the autumn of 1972. Perfect balance and a great tactical awareness had been added to his natural feel for horses. Saint-Martin honed his skills against the likes of Jean Deforge and Roger Poincelet, themselves marvellous riders. "It was a very good school for me because I competed against many great jockeys – it was very hard to win for an apprentice with no experience." He also owed much to the powerful Mathet stable for whom he had ridden 13 of his classic winners by 1973 and, indeed, an awful lot to the trainer himself. "Mathet and me is like father and the little boy," he has said. "He taught me everything but he never allow my opinions." The former cavalry officer's autocratic mien caused them to split during the 1970s but their eventual reunion was crowned by further classic triumphs with Topville (1979 French Derby) and Melyno (1982 French 1,000 Guineas) and an Arc success with Akiyada in 1982.

In his initial 6-year association with Wildenstein's horses during the 1970s Saint-Martin won 23 Group I races in France alone in addition to 3 classics and a King George in England (he rejoined Wildenstein to win 3 more in the 1980s). The majority of these were on fillies though Saint-Martin denies any special affinity with the fairer sex. "Fillies in filly races, colts in colt races, all the same." Allez France's contribution was 8 – Criterium des Pouliches at 2, the Poule d'Essai des Pouliches (1,000 Guineas), Prix de Diane

(Oaks), Prix Vermeille at 3, Prix de l'Arc de Triomphe, Prix Ganay, Prix d'Ispahan at 4 and the Ganay a second time at 5, the last 4 of which were, significantly, versus colts.

It was Allez France's destiny to beat the colts and prove herself the best in Europe but not in 1973. She ran 7 times, only once out of Group I company, and won the 3 premier fillies events. The Poule d'Essai des Pouliches was almost a case of déja vu – the same course and distance as the Criterium, the same apparently hopeless position at the head of the straight, the same instantaneous response once a gap materialized through which Saint-Martin could send her. On the strength of this display she was installed favourite for the Epsom Derby, a race seldom contested by fillies since the war despite the 5lb allowance. The last to win was Fifinella in a 1916 wartime substitute at Newmarket (in 1975 the French filly Nobiliary would finish second to Grundy). However, Allez France never got to Epsom. After she finished out of the first 6 to the French 2,000 Guineas winner Kalamoun in the 1¼-mile Prix Lupin it was assumed she would not stay the Derby distance and she was withdrawn in favour of a crack at the shorter Prix de Diane.

Any doubts regarding Allez France's stamina were dispelled at Chantilly as Saint-Martin, enjoying a clear passage for once, brought her away from the remainder to shatter the race record even though the ground was on the soft side. Second place was occupied by Dahlia who nearly fell on the turn and who would frank the winner's quality by winning the Irish Oaks and the King George inside the next month. Allez France had now beaten Dahlia twice (she had been third in the Guineas) and would do so again on 5 other occasions.

When the partnership resumed action after a 12-week break the result proved sensational. In the Prix de la Nonnette they finished in front of only their 2 pacemakers. Ring-rustiness must have been the cause since 3 weeks later Allez France thrashed the first 3 when they reopposed her in the Prix Vermeille. The Irish filly Hurry Harriet was second and Dahlia, who finished lame after slipping, fifth. This was truly a mighty performance from Allez France and augured well for the Arc and her second confrontation with colts, who this time would be of all ages. Only the previous season the Vermeille winner San San had gone on to win the Arc in the hands of Saint-Martin. However, this was not fated to be Allez France's year. She started 7/4 favourite but the English four-year-old colt Rheingold, ridden by Lester Piggott, stole first run and held her determined challenge by 2½ lengths. A trip abroad – her first – for the Champion Stakes likewise ended in failure. "I am in front, I go in front easy," says Saint-Martin in faltering English, "but she stop to look at the stand. In Newmarket it is very special with the stands right on the course – she look, she stop!" Hurry Harriet,

Allez France and Angel Penna

whom she had defeated in the Vermeille and Arc got up to beat her $\frac{3}{4}$ length. As in the Nonnette this was not the real Allez France. The 4 fillies to beat her in 1973 were all put in their rightful place at one time or another.

If Allez France and Saint-Martin came close to immortality in 1973 they more than made amends in 1974, winning each and every one of their 5 outings (all at Longchamp) culminating with the Arc on October 6th. One new face appeared in Allez France's throng of male devotees. Albert Klimscha had retired and Angel Penna, who had trained Le Chouan for the Wildensteins in the United States, now assumed control of their French horses.

Born in Buenos Aires in 1923, Angel Penna never had any doubts that he would follow his father as a trainer of racehorses. By 1946 he had established himself as a public trainer and was leading trainer from 1947 until he moved to Venezuela in 1954. There also he became champion trainer. Thirteen years on, he transferred to the United States, enjoying notable successes with Bold Reason and Czar Alexander before arriving in France to train for Countess Margit Batthyany at Lamorlaye. His first runner, the filly Mata Hari, was a winner and a month later she gave him the first of his 7 French and English classic victories by taking the French 1,000 Guineas. As 6 of these 7 classics came from fillies (besides a King George, Champion, two Vermeilles and two Arcs) it seems safe to assert that Penna had a way with ladies. He was now afforded the opportunity of working with the greatest filly seen in Europe since the war.

Allez France and Saint-Martin scarcely encountered one hiccup in their run-up to the Arc. Making their seasonal bow in mid-April they proceeded to win 3 races inside 6 weeks, the Prix d'Harcourt by 3 lengths (Dahlia fourth), the Ganay by 5 lengths (Dahlia defeated for the sixth time) and the Prix d'Ispahan by a casual 1 length. In all 3 they started odds on and, moreover, walloped the colts. The Ganay and d'Ispahan were especially spectacular with Saint-Martin keeping her on the bridle as long as prudently possible. In the latter she was all of 15 lengths adrift 2 furlongs out but literally tore up the straight. The notion of raiding Ascot for the King George was laid aside in favour of a mid-summer rest prior to a preparatory race for the Arc. The Prix Foy safely won, there only remained the Arc 4 weeks later.

Then came the slight hiccup. Ten days before the big day Saint-Martin broke a small bone at the top of his thigh when his mount in a lowly Maisons-Laffitte handicap unseated him in the paddock. There was talk of Lester Piggott switching to Allez France from arch rival Dahlia (who did not run in the end) but Saint-Martin refused to abandon "his filly" on the eve of her toughest examination. Swimming, massage and, finally 90 minutes before the off, a pain-killing injection, saw him through. "I don't walk, I come to the racetrack on sticks but the start was delayed for television and just after the finish of the race – voom – the finish of the injection! It was terrible, when I take off my saddle. In the jockeys' room I change, I take my stick and I go and sleep for 3 weeks. To ride that race was the most important thing."

Drawn 15 of the 20 runners toward the outside, Saint-Martin had little option but drop Allez France in behind the pack. However, so smoothly was she travelling on the final bend that she swept into the lead and appeared likely to coast home. Then out of the ruck shot Comtesse de Loir. Disaster seemed imminent until Allez France displayed a brand of courage to match that of her patched-up partner. "Most women are a lot braver than most men in terms of pain which a racehorse endures at the heat of battle," insists Penna. "They are innately more stoic than we. The secret is to make them want to do their best for you. A great one will not let you down." Saint-Martin knew the secret all right; Allez France was a great one. Together they responded to the upstart filly and to the undisguised joy of the 39,000 crowd it was the distinctive white noseband of Allez France that reached the post first. The winning margin was a head.

Saint-Martin later explained that Allez France struck the front far earlier than he had intended but after being pushed to the outside by one of her opponents she flew at this premature sign of daylight. This victory made Allez France the first horse in European history to earn over £450,000 in win and place money, though Dahlia was soon to surpass that figure largely as a result of a successful campaign in North America.

Allez France stayed in training with the aim of landing a second Arc but although she apparently waltzed through her first 2 races of 1975 – the Ganay (beating Comtesse de Loir, Hurry Harriet and Dahlia) and Prix Dollar – a little of the old zip was missing. She was beaten 2 lengths into third in the d'Ispahan but a facile victory in the Prix Foy did not preface Arc success on this occasion. Allez France finished fifth, some $8\frac{1}{2}$ lengths behind the surprise winner Star Appeal, after suffering interference which gave her a nasty cut and wrenched off her near hind shoe. A fortnight later she reversed the form with Star Appeal in the Champion Stakes though still found the English filly Rose Bowl $1\frac{1}{2}$ lengths too good on the day.

This pair of defeats suggested the Allez France of old had gone forever. A third defeat in the National Thoroughbred Championship run on dirt at Santa Anita, California in November was needless, based as it was round an attempt upon Dahlia's world record earnings for a mare. Penna realized deep down that Allez France required a miracle to win a race of this kind and yet he kept wondering whether she could do it for him one final time.

"A great one will not let you down" – Allez France wins the Arc

His prayers went unanswered. The race was a nightmare for all who knew the authentic article. "She was just a shadow of herself," says Penna. "It broke my heart to watch her lose. It was the saddest day of my life."

She and Saint-Martin finished last of the 11 runners behind the Argentinian mare Dulcia. "She is tired, tired, she is gone – she don't like the sand," is all Saint-Martin can say about this sad finale to the illustrious career of a filly whom he describes as "fantastic, special – the top horse in my jockey's life." Their 13 victories had earned £493,100.

Allez France stayed in the land of her birth to be mated with the 1973 American Triple Crown hero Secretariat. Why bother, mused Penna, for you won't breed another Secretariat or Allez France however hard you try. Similarly, you cannot manufacture the brand of magic with which Allez France and Yves Saint-Martin mesmerised the Longchamp faithful, for it comes from the heart.

Allez France enters her box to be met by her friend the sheep

ALLEZ FRANCE

Bay filly 1970
Ran 21   Won 13   Placed 4   Value of Races Won £493,100

Allez France	Sea-Bird II	Dan Cupid	Native Dancer / Vixenette
		Sicalade	Sicambre / Marmelade
	Priceless Gem	Hail to Reason	Turn-to / Nothirdchance
		Searching	War Admiral / Big Hurry

TEN

Nagwa and Ray Cochrane

As 1986 drew to a close jockey Ray Cochrane could reflect on his finest ever season. A career high total of 89 winners included his first classic success on Midway Lady in the 1,000 Guineas and Oaks and undoubtedly helped him to land the prestigious retainer as stable jockey to Luca Cumani. The 28-year-old Ulsterman had come a long way since the day in 1972 when he arrived at Lambourn to commence his apprenticeship with Barry Hills. The road had not been exactly uneventful. He enjoyed a successful apprenticeship but when his right to claim was up and he had no allowance to "sell", the telephone stopped ringing. "I went from riding 3 or 4 horses a day to 3 a week. Also I began to get heavy." The climb back was fraught with difficulty and demanded considerable perseverence and dedication. August 1977 saw him riding over hurdles (he rode 8 winners altogether) and he spent a season working for Fred Winter. However, with 5 ahead of him in the queue for rides at Uplands he upped sticks and joined Ron Sheather in Newmarket.

The breakthrough occurred in June 1983 when he got the mount on Sheather's big black juvenile Chief Singer and the pairing won the Coventry, St James's Palace, July Cup and Sussex Stakes during the ensuing 14 months. Then, in 1986, along came Midway Lady. However, when he said, "I don't think I'll ever get another like her to ride," Cochrane was not referring to his dual classic winner. He spoke those words on dismounting from a sparely-made two-year-old filly called Nagwa after winning a £690 6-furlong plate at Leicester on October 20th 1975. Eleven years later he saw no reason to alter that sentiment. "No matter how many good horses you ride she was the sort that sets you alight – a really lovable sort of filly – and I'll never forget her."

Nagwa and Cochrane were a true partnership. Neither were stars; to achieve fame they needed each other. Nagwa was a good 7lb below the top fillies of her generation and therefore benefited from Cochrane's allowance while the young Irishman was on the verge of quitting Lambourn due to a lack of rides.

> "One Sunday I plucked up courage to see the guv'nor and told him that I was going on a week's holiday and that if things were unlikely to change I wasn't coming back. Needless to say I received a terrific rollocking and was put firmly in my place. However the next day I was given a ride on Lord Helpus at Leicester and just got beat a short head. Soon after that I was told I could ride Nagwa for the rest of the season."

When Cochrane partnered Nagwa for the first time in Chepstow's Morning West Nursery on August 25th it was only his eighth ride of the season and he had just one victory to his credit, on Court Melody in an apprentice handicap at Newbury. Yet after 18 more rides his 1986 winning percentage climbed to a remarkable 38.46 thanks to 9 victories on Nagwa from 10 starts. By contrast the champion jockey Pat Eddery could only boast a percentage of 20.10.

In consequence Nagwa established a 20th-century record for two-year-old victories with a total of 13, 3 less than The Bard's all-time figure of 16 set in 1885 (later equalled by Provideo in 1984). The chemistry between Nagwa and Cochrane contained more than a trace of the sublime. She was not considered the easiest of rides, being naturally idle and in need of constant driving. "Previously she'd always been ridden along from the start but I liked to give her a chance to find her legs, let her relax and build up into the race," is how Cochrane explains the formula, though he is quick to admit, "the 7lb allowance did no harm either!" That Nagwa was extremely tough could not be denied. In all she competed in 20 races, beginning on May 2nd, concluding on November 3rd, and during the last 2 months of the season when most early-season types are being demobilised, she turned out on 10 occasions including 2 races in 3 days at York and Catterick.

Bred by the Tsarina Stud in County Limerick, Nagwa was purchased for 6,200 guineas as a yearling by Kalifa Sasi. Pronounced "Narjwa" her Arabic name roughly translates to "Whisper of Lovers". She was a bay by the sprinter/miler Tower Walk, who won the July Cup, Nunthorpe and Prix de l'Abbaye in the late 1960s, and the first foal of Tamarisk, herself a sprinter, who won at Yarmouth as a juvenile in 1970. Tamarisk hated heavy ground and often required strong handling to be seen to her best advantage, traits she passed to her daughter. Nagwa's grandam My Dream, on the other hand, showed far superior class, winning the 1961 Queen Mary Stakes at Royal Ascot.

Nagwa was no beauty. "She was not too small," says Cochrane, "but rather plain and scrawny. She also had a very scratchy action and was a terrible

Nagwa and Ray Cochrane

trotter. However in a race she was a perfect ride, very intelligent and knew all about racing. Nagwa might not have been much to look at but she could sure win races."

Barry Hills introduced her to racing in the Wilbraham Maiden Plate at the Newmarket Guineas Meeting. Ridden by Willie Carson, Nagwa showed her inexperience by swerving left on leaving the gate and, as a result, running out of puff in the last 2 furlongs to finish fourth to the 7/4 favourite Get Ready, beaten a total of 5 lengths. This was no disgrace for a debut effort and there was some stable confidence behind her when she was sent up to York for a similar event 11 days later. Again she found the favourite, Everything Nice, just her better after disputing the lead for most of the race and indeed taking a fractional advantage at the distance. Watching from the grandstand was Ray Cochrane, waiting to ride Bold Picture in the last race of the day in which he would come fifth in a blanket finish, less than $\frac{3}{4}$ length covering the first 7 horses.

Nagwa's attentions were next directed to Haydock and on the strength of her form to date she was made an odds-on favourite to win her maiden at the third attempt. Three failed to be a lucky number and she was run out of the prize in the final furlong. It was beginning to look as if Nagwa would be the eternal bridesmaid. Not for the first time a rest and a change of jockey broke the spell. Ernie Johnson had an armchair ride as Nagwa won Leicester's Huncote Maiden Stakes on June 16th by 3 lengths. With the hoodoo lifted Nagwa promptly ran up a sequence of 3 more victories (2 with Johnson, 1 with Carson) at Brighton, Haydock and Redcar by mid-July.

If the truth be told Nagwa did not have an awful lot to beat in these contests and she started odds-on each time. Her next race would be altogether a different proposition. The Princess Margaret Stakes on the day of Ascot's King George & Queen Elizabeth Stakes always attracts one or two of the crack early-season fillies and 1975 proved no exception. In a select field of four Nagwa started a warm favourite but 2 of her rivals held smart form, namely Ian Balding's Newbury winner Outer Circle and Peter Walwyn's Blue Waffles, a winner at Sandown. Although she led nearing the finish Nagwa was ultimately worn down by Outer Circle and capitulated by a head. Before the two met again in the Cheveley Park, Outer Circle won Ripon's Champion Trophy to confirm her above-average ability.

This defeat in the highest class might be excused but another in a Redcar Nursery in early August could not. Admittedly she conceded 26lb to her conqueror Dutch Martyr yet the task ought to have been within her compass. If she was unable to trouble the elite fillies then contests of this sort might become her bread and butter, in which case an apprentice rider would prove a priceless asset. Accordingly Ray Cochrane's plea for more opportunities reaped dividends since he got the ride in Chepstow's valuable Morning West Nursery Handicap.

Born in Gilford, County Down, Cochrane's first equine encounter came at home when jumping on the back of an old carthorse from a tree. "From then on I always wanted to be a jockey." The local riding school provided the threshold to a future career and progress was so rapid that he was soon acting as tutor rather than student. "I was there for 5 years and gained a lot of experience with horses and people. If you can deal with both in this game then it's a bonus. The horses aren't always the awkward ones! Eventually I decided there was more scope in England and after trying Frenchie Nicholson, who was chock-a-block as usual, and a few others, it was Barry Hills who said I could come." Consequently in 1972 the 14-year-old Cochrane arrived at South Bank Stables in Lambourn. However, the eagerly-sought rides failed to materialise, prompting him to adopt those desperate measures of Sunday August 17th 1975.

Cochrane's 7lb allowance reduced Nagwa's Chepstow weight to 8st 13lb and though she had to give away at least a stone to the other 6 runners they were of so little account that she and her young partner galloped home effortlessly by 4 lengths.

On the final day of September the duo began their concerted assault on the record books which brought them 8 victories in 2 months. First they journeyed north to Pontefract, not a venue synonymous with historic deeds. Cochrane had not ridden here before and approaching the turn he and Nagwa had got themselves boxed-in along the rail. Fortunately the brick-hard ground caused the field to negotiate the bend so fast that the leaders swung wide allowing Cochrane to force Nagwa up the inside. The moment of crisis passed and the rest was straightforward as Nagwa comfortably beat Henry Cecil's dual winner Great Idea by $1\frac{1}{2}$ lengths. Once more the wisdom of utilizing Cochrane was vindicated since his allowance ensured Nagwa received a vital 6lb from the second instead of conceding 1lb. Five days later the circumstances were repeated in Thirsk's Highflyer Stakes because the filly beat Short Reign by 3 lengths in receipt of 7lb after the deduction of Cochrane's allowance.

Nagwa then travelled to the other end of the country to run in Folkestone's Danes Stakes in which she again trounced Short Reign, this time at only a 2lb weight difference. Luckily she never turned a hair when travelling. Cochrane always accompanied Nagwa, and her lass Zita, in the horsebox.

"She was a very sensible old thing. You wouldn't know she was in the box and she thrived on racing. All she did was eat, sleep, travel and race. I never rode her at home. If she did work one of the Hills twins usually rode her. Mostly

Nagwa winning the Junior Plate at Pontefract

I'd just lead her out into the paddock third lot to let her have a pick of grass or occasionally trot her up the road."

After a break of 2 weeks that must have resembled a holiday to Nagwa she resumed active service at Redcar in the 7-furlong Tally-Ho Stakes, her first attempt at the distance. The outcome proved memorable although to begin with the venture appeared doomed. Cochrane recalls:

"I was not happy with her when we arrived at Redcar the evening before the race. She gave the odd cough, was a bit dull in her coat and had a dirty nose. We cleaned up her nose, put some Vick on it, and waited to see how she'd be on the Saturday. She seemed all right but if not the Guv'nor told me to be easy on her."

The ground was very firm and they set off at a tremendous lick headed by old adversary Great Idea who had won at Yarmouth since the Pontefract race. By halfway even the indolent Nagwa was off the bit, a very unusual occurrence, yet as soon as Cochrane clucked in her ear she veritably exploded into action and stormed clear of the remainder. At the post 5 lengths separated her from Partridge Brook. The clock stopped at 1 minute 21.90, an enormous 2.4 seconds inside the old two-year-old track record for 7 furlongs and, incredibly, some $\frac{1}{2}$ second faster than the all-aged best for the distance. There are some who decry the validity of track records due to their tendency to be set mostly on firm ground but the sheer majesty of Nagwa's display reinforced the clock's insistence that she had accomplished a remarkable performance.

Faced with continual evidence of Nagwa's improvement Barry Hills decided to pitch her back into the highest class and chose the Cheveley Park for her next outing. Among the 13 opponents were Pasty, the unbeaten winner of 4 races including the Lowther and Lavant; the Irish filly Petipa; Hayloft, winner of the Molecomb, and Outer Circle. Being a Group I event Cochrane could not claim his 7lb and not surprisingly in view of the race's significance he gave way to Willie Carson. "I was not too concerned about it because I'd had so little experience beyond Nagwa."

The larger than average field for such a championship race confirmed the belief that no really outstanding filly had emerged during the summer. Petipa started favourite with Nagwa fifth best at tens but her deadliest opponent turned out to be the soft ground which she met for the first time. The conclusion was indeed a close one of necks and heads – 4 lengths covered the first 10 – but Nagwa was not involved. She finished tenth, 6 lengths off the leader, a total misrepresentation of her merits.

However, reunited with Cochrane she had 4 more victories to come, at York (by far her most lucrative at £1,335, on October 11th), Catterick (October 18th), Leicester (October 20th) and Lingfield (November 3rd), interrupted only by a single reverse at Teeside on October 27th. "The Teeside defeat was all my fault," admits her jockey. "By now I was beginning to think we were unbeatable. Well, we missed the gate and a very fast animal called Delayed Action got away from us. I could never quite get to him and we got beat a neck."

The Catterick race still holds a vivid place in Cochrane's memory since it was the first occasion he rode in a match. His solitary rival in the 6-furlong Ilkley Stakes was the Cecil-trained Corriefeol, a winner at Doncaster and Yarmouth, who had finished in front of Nagwa on their Newmarket debut. This day she conceded 7lb and had not raced for 2 months, causing Nagwa's superior fitness to assume the key factor. Cochrane, reasoning that Alan Bond on Corriefeol would try to sit on his tail and beat him for speed, formulated his tactics accordingly.

"I decided to go to the front at my own speed and let him try to beat me. I planned to eventually look over my right shoulder, knowing that as soon as I did Alan would immediately come the other side. So, as I took a glance $1\frac{1}{2}$ furlongs out, I went for the line. We won by $\frac{3}{4}$ length. It's always sweet when the pre-planning works to perfection, especially in a situation I'd not experienced before.''

The Nagwa–Cochrane relationship had by now attracted detailed attention from the press. "Queen Nagwa the Eleventh," declared *The Sporting Life* after this victory. Two days later the *Life* gave her twelfth success in Leicester's Cottesmore Plate more exposure than customarily granted small affairs. Nagwa won comfortably enough by 2 lengths but, at last feeling the effects of her hard season, she needed to be roused in the closing stages. The Teeside defeat appeared to signal the end of her exertions but the prospect of a place in the record books attracted her to Lingfield at the beginning of November for the 7-furlong Plaistow Plate, some 6 months and 19 races after her debut. Furthermore, the going was soft and despite Cochrane's allowance Nagwa had to give weight to all the others. She very nearly failed to last out the trip in the circumstances and only managed to repel the Frank Durr partnered Steel Power by a rapidly diminishing head. "I could hear Frank's whip swishing and a few strides past the post he came by me.''

The record safely secured, Nagwa deservedly went out to grass. Thirteen wins had earned a measly £9,100, not much more than second prize in the Cheveley Park, a rating of 8st 5lb in the Free Handicap (8lb below the top filly Pasty) and a debt of eternal gratitude from Ray Cochrane. "She was a lovely little thing, the type everyone likes to ride and be associated with.''

Nagwa was sold to go to North America while Cochrane fought his way out of the wilderness to achieve classic glory in 1986.

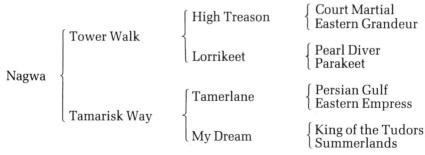

NAGWA

Brown filly 1973
Ran 20   Won 13   Placed 5   Value of Races Won £9,100

Nagwa	Tower Walk	High Treason	Court Martial / Eastern Grandeur
		Lorrikeet	Pearl Diver / Parakeet
	Tamarisk Way	Tamerlane	Persian Gulf / Eastern Empress
		My Dream	King of the Tudors / Summerlands

ELEVEN

Genuine Risk and Jacinto Vasquez

Seldom do fillies challenge the colts for the American classic races of Kentucky Derby, Preakness and Belmont. American horsemen consider the three-year-old filly far too delicate and fragile to compete with the male of the species at this stage of her development and there are, after all, sufficient fat purses elsewhere in races confined to her own sex. In the 105 years of its existence prior to 1980 only one filly, Regret in 1915, had ever won the Kentucky Derby and 21 years elapsed since a filly had even competed in the event (Silver Spoon, fifth in 1959). Consequently when Genuine Risk passed under the wire first in the 1980 renewal of the "Run for the Roses" she created one of the upsets of the century in American racing. "Fillies are supposed to die," commented one of the beaten jockeys, "they're not supposed to run like that at $1\frac{1}{4}$ miles." Fortunately for Genuine Risk her connections harboured no such prejudice against mixed-sex racing, preferring to place their faith in the law of the wild where it is the lioness who hunts, protects, fights and competes while the lion is the one who lies around looking pretty.

The jockey aboard Genuine Risk was neither a stranger to sensational results nor great fillies. Back in 1973 Jacinto Vasquez partnered both Angle Light and Onion to individual victories over the Triple Crown winner Secretariat ("I'll make the Hall of Fame yet, beating these famous horses," he quipped) and 3 years later was associated with Ruffian, the filly with blistering pace who was unbeaten in 10 races until tragically breaking a leg in a match-race at Belmont. If another romantic ingredient is added to the story in the form of Genuine Risk's purchase as a yearling at the Fasig-Tipton Sales of 1978, one is left with no alternative but to believe in fairy tales.

Genuine Risk ran in the colours of Mrs Diana Firestone, the wife of Bertram Firestone, owner of the Cilltown Stud in Ireland and the Catoctin Stud in Virginia. The couple had been incredibly lucky with their sales purchases, the colts like Kentucky Derby second Honest Pleasure (cost $45,000, won

$839,997) running in Bert's name and the fillies such as Kentucky Oaks winner Optimistic Gal (cost $55,000, won $686,000) in that of Diana. On this side of the Atlantic, Kings Company (1971) and Flash of Steel (1986) won the Irish 2,000 Guineas and Blue Wind the English and Irish Oaks of 1981.

In this light it comes as no surprise to learn that Genuine Risk was not home-bred and therein lies the tale. In the summer of 1978 the Firestones' 14-year-old son Matthew was working at the Fasig-Tipton Sales in Kentucky, as he had done for several years, grooming and walking yearlings for Dr Smiser West's Waterford Farm. As the sale progressed Matthew's enthusiasm grew for a bright chestnut filly adorned with a broad white blaze and 1 white sock on her near-hind. "This is the first horse I've actually gone and picked," he confessed after the Derby. "I looked at her and she seemed like a filly who could run." Despite considerable bullying on Matthew's part it was only on the night she was due to be sold that father Bert and his trainer LeRoy Jolley consented to examine the yearling. Even at this point Firestone hesitated, wondering whether the consignors would pull out the filly for inspection so close to the auction but his son's insistence paid off. They estimated the filly would fetch $35,000. "We talked about it and Dad said we could work out a loan and I got her for $32,000."

Besides her looks young Firestone had been attracted by the presence of classic winners Gallant Man and Tomy Lee on the distaff side of her pedigree. The former lost the 1957 Kentucky Derby by a nose after Bill Shoemaker misjudged the finish line and stood up in the irons but made amends by winning the Belmont by 8 lengths in record time. Two years later Shoemaker judged the location of the wire at Churchill Downs to perfection when driving home Tomy Lee to win the Derby.

Genuine Risk was by Exclusive Native out of the Gallant Man mare Virtuous who belonged to the Auld Alliance (the dam of Tomy Lee) and thus traced to the English Derby winner Ocean Swell. Virtuous raced in France and the United States, winning 2 of her 10 races. The next dam, Due Respect, won 2 small races in England and was Tomy Lee's half-sister. She also threw the useful sprinter Shoolerville who won the Vernons Sprint Trial when trained by Sam Armstrong. Exclusive Native did not win a classic himself but his son Affirmed won all 3 in 1978 and he had compiled an impressive record in his first 6 years at stud.

Genuine Risk was bred by Mrs Sally Humphrey at Shawnee Farm, near Harrodsburg, some 20 miles south west of Lexington. Her husband Watts inherited the farm upon the death of his aunt Mrs Parker Poe who used to campaign horses like Young Emperor and La Tendresse with Paddy Prendergast. Mrs Humphrey bought Virtuous for $31,500 at the 1975 Keeneland

Genuine Risk

November Breeding Stock auction. Each year she received a certain amount of money from her husband to spend on a mare in lieu of a birthday present. Virtuous was Sally Humphrey's 30th birthday present. At the time of purchase Virtuous was in foal to Stage Door Johnny and Genuine Risk was her second offspring.

Like most of the Firestones' American stock Genuine Risk was subsequently sent to John Nazareth, who combined the job of Jolley's Assistant Trainer with the managership of the St Lucy Training Centre at West Palm Beach in Florida where, from November to April, he broke yearlings on a freelance basis. Dahlia, for one, was broken here. He remembers Genuine Risk as a very kind, relaxed and feminine individual, not a big filly but a versatile one.

Bucked shins delayed Genuine Risk's debut until late September of 1979 but she then racked up 4 victories in 7 weeks including the Grade III Tempted Stakes and Grade II Demoiselle Stakes at Aqueduct. On dismounting after the 1-mile Tempted, her first success, Vasquez looked LeRoy Jolley straight in the eye and said, "This filly will win next year's Derby," – some statement for the jockey to make given the accepted non-participation of fillies in the race! Vasquez's words were either fuelled by hot air or startling perception. During the winter months, while the filly rested, Firestone and Jolley began to seriously consider the jockey's advice.

Born in Las Tablas, Panama, the 36-year-old Vasquez, jockey-room practical joker and checkers king, now regarded himself as an adopted New Yorker. He began his riding career at the age of 13 and rode his first winner at 15. A year later he hit New York and was now well past the 3,000 winner mark in a career which numbered big wins with Loud (1970) and General Assembly (1979) in the Travers Stakes, Proud Birdie (1977) in the Marlboro Cup and Angle Light in that Wood Memorial of 1973. However, in the minds of the Firestones, of greater significance was the fact that in 1975 he had won the Kentucky Derby on Foolish Pleasure (trained by Jolley) and been linked with the immortal, though ill-fated, filly Ruffian. Besides her, Vasquez had won Grade I events on other superb fillies like Furl Sail in 1967, Bundler in 1973 and Revidere in 1976.

Thus it was quite conceivable that Vasquez knew exactly what he was talking about when he claimed Genuine Risk would win the Derby. The Firestones' familiarity with European racing where three-year-old fillies regularly compete against the colts made them far more receptive to the idea than most Americans. In short, the more they mulled over the notion the more it appealed to them.

Once Genuine Risk reappeared in March to gain easy victories against her own sex over 7 furlongs and a mile at Gulfstream and Aqueduct the nettle had to be grasped. It was decided to start her against the colts in the Wood Memorial, the traditional trial run 2 Saturdays before the Derby at Aqueduct, where she would clash with Plugged Nickle, winner of the Florida Derby and ante post favourite for the classic. The colt won with the filly 1½ lengths and a head behind in third, but he drifted into her path as she tried to make a run in the final furlong and Vasquez lodged an objection. As if to imply that it was a rough game when you played with the boys and there must be no squealing from any females unwise enough to join in, the objection was overruled.

Genuine Risk's participation at Churchill Downs now assumed "will-she-won't-she" proportions. Jolley favoured resting her with a view to the New York fillies' triple later in the summer. Firestone, on the other hand, was prepared to clutch at any straw offering her a chance of success and announced that no final decision would be made until after the Blue Grass Stakes, the last recognized trial held 9 days before the Derby, in which Prince Valiant, the colt he feared most, was due to run. Prince Valiant ran deplorably finishing last behind the gelding Rockhill Native and was withdrawn from the classic. Also, the field which had looked likely at one stage to exceed 30 shrank to half that, thereby eliminating the possibility of a bargeing match. Suitably encouraged Firestone had Genuine Risk shipped to Kentucky. Vasquez would get the chance to justify his prophecy.

Some considered the Firestones insane to pass up a certain $100,000 purse in the Kentucky Oaks just to take a fling at the Derby. Diana Firestone was well prepared for such attacks. "At Navan last week we ran a three-year-old filly who gave 10lb to a colt and got beaten a neck," to which husband Bert added, "If we'd done that in America they'd have sent for the men in white coats to come and quietly take us away." However the Firestones were not totally out on a limb. The previous season John Veitch trained the brilliant filly Davona Dale. She had twice taken on the colts unsuccessfully but as Veitch pointed out, unlike his champion, Genuine Risk had no Affirmed or Spectacular Bid to defeat and was a worthy contender.

Arguably Genuine Risk's credentials were the best in the race for although the 10 colts and 2 geldings completing the field were a respectable bunch the 1980 Derby seemed to lack superstars such as Spectacular Bid, Affirmed and Seattle Slew who had won the last 3 renewals. The first 3 in the Blue Grass were naturally here as was Plugged Nickle. The Californian challenge was led by Rumbo, runner-up in both the Santa Anita and Hollywood Derbies to Codex, who owing to some sort of oversight had not been nominated for the Kentucky Derby. Nicknamed "Dumbo" because of his erratic, playful behaviour and his recent disinclination to pass the last horse, the former would have the assistance of Laffit Pincay in the saddle.

Despite possessing form the equal of any colt in the field Genuine Risk was allowed to start at the remunerative odds of 13/1. Only 8 of the 101 reporters who entered the annual Derby selection contest opted for her. Few took notice of her workout earlier in the week when she covered 5 furlongs 2 seconds faster than Rockhill Native, whom the horseplayers now made favourite. Vasquez kept the filly calm during the traditional pre-race razzamatazz even when the aptly named Degenerate John nearly trod on her in the paddock.

The gates clanged open and Vasquez immediately settled the filly in the middle of the pack but toward the outer where she could expect a trouble-free journey. The favourite took them along at a slowish pace by American standards. If the gelding were to win he would be greeted with a reception and a place in history almost on a par with that awaiting Genuine Risk, since no gelding had triumphed since Clyde Van Dusen in 1929. However entering the stretch, "she went on and my horse just kind of laid there," said the favourite's crestfallen rider, Oldham. Pounding down the centre

Genuine Risk and Jacinto Vasquez winning the Kentucky Derby

of the track Genuine Risk headed for the wire and a slice of history and
although Rumbo came out of the ruck to reduce the gap and thus maintain
his irritating sequence of seconds, she still had a length in hand at the
death. The authority of the filly's powerful surge to an epic victory was
emphasized by the clock, possibly a more meaningful criterion of excellence
on the homogenous tracks of America than anywhere else in the world.
In spite of the tardy early gallop her time of 2 minutes 02.00 seconds was
faster than that of either Spectacular Bid or Affirmed.

Vasquez and Genuine Risk had confounded those jeremiahs who doubted
the filly's ability to outfight the colts. "You can't take anything away from
her," admitted trainer Tommy Kelly whose Plugged Nickle trailed in a disappointing seventh, "She's a helluva nice filly." As it happened Plugged Nickle
was the sole adversary with some kind of excuse – he returned with a cut
near hind – but all in all it was a result that had to be swallowed whether
or not it stuck in the throat.

Having succumbed to one temptation it was not unreasonable that Bert Firestone would find irresistible the far greater temptation of a tilt at the Preakness (won by 4 fillies) and Belmont (won by 2), that is a shot at the Triple Crown. "That really would be history," he declared. Vasquez, never devoid of confidence, had no qualms concerning her ability to stay the trip in the Belmont. "With this competition she'll go 2 miles," were his thoughts on the subject.

Nevertheless the competition at Pimlico for the Preakness 2 weeks later would be augmented by the presence of Codex, who on a line through Rumbo, could claim to be at least the filly's equal. If the story of Genuine Risk was a fairy tale it came to an abrupt, unhappy end in the Preakness and the villain of the piece was irrefutable – Angel Cordero, the rider of Codex.

Third for the initial $\frac{1}{2}$ mile Codex moved to the fore with barely 3 furlongs to travel but veered noticeably toward the centre of the track necessitating a right-hand whip from Cordero. Meanwhile Genuine Risk, who had already once momentarily lost her action down the back stretch, drew alongside rounding the final turn, only to be the recipient of every crime in the book if Vasquez's post race comments are to be believed. The 2 horses did appear to brush at the top of the straight and the filly did return sporting a large bump under her left eye but whether this was caused by Cordero slashing her across the snout, as Vasquez claimed, could not accurately be ascertained even with the camera's aid. The stewards had no option but to overrule Vasquez's objection, particularly as the colt's superiority eventually totalled 4 lengths. The supposition that any interference had no material effect on the race's outcome weighed significantly in the stewards' minds and though Firestone filed a petition with the Maryland Racing Commission and the debate raged across the country for days courtesy of coast-to-coast television, the result was upheld.

Although Genuine Risk's attempt on the Preakness, and thus the Triple Crown, may have failed there was still the Belmont, on June 7th, in which she could take revenge on Codex. On a muddy track exact revenge she did but that second classic victory eluded her as she was beaten 2 lengths by Temperance Hill (the only horse to wear mud-calks). He had won the Arkansas Derby back in April before proving no match for Colonel Moran (whom Genuine Risk beat in the Preakness) in the Withers Stakes. Subsequent events suggested Temperance Hill had 2 distinct ways of running. On his good days he could beat John Henry in the Jockey Club Gold Cup whereas he contrived to lose 3 in a row after the Belmont.

Thus at the conclusion of the 1980 classic series Genuine Risk had to content herself with being the only filly to reach the frame in all 3. An achievement of this magnitude could not pass unrecognized, however, and she was voted champion filly while the magazine *Harper's Bazaar* took the unprecedented step of numbering her among the list of "Top Seven Women Achievers" of the year, giving as the reason for this singular honour that "the filly's name reminded women of what is required by the best – a willingness to chance the odds". In addition Genuine Risk was later elected to the Racing Hall of Fame at the National Museum of Racing at Saratoga Springs.

The historic partnership between Genuine Risk and Jacinto Vasquez did not end at Belmont. After a long rest the filly resumed in the autumn and contested a titanic race for the Maskette Handicap Stakes on September 10th against the other superb filly of her generation Bold 'N Determined, who had won 2 of the 3 races that constitute the New York Racing Association's Fillies Triple Crown, and Davona Dale who had won all 3 the previous season. Those 3 severe battles against the colts now took their toll as Bold 'N Determined won by a nose. Genuine Risk was back to her very best for the Grade I Ruffian Handicap and, much to Vasquez's delight, won the race named in honour of his former mount by a nose from Misty Gallore. They won more races in 1981, bringing their record to 10 wins from 15 starts (never having run unplaced) before Genuine Risk was retired to Catoctin.

"She is an extremely smart and intelligent filly," maintains Diana Firestone. "She seems to be completely relaxed and thoroughly enjoys her regular exercise as though she really appreciates being part of our daily lives." A magnificent bronze depicting Genuine Risk bearing her Derby garland of honour is one of the Firestones' proudest possessions. It is appropriately entitled "Her Finest Hour" and is a constant reminder of the never-to-be-forgotten day when Genuine Risk and Jacinto Vasquez put the colts in their place by winning the Run for the Roses.

GENUINE RISK

Chestnut filly 1977
Ran 15   Won 10   Placed 5   Value of Races Won $646,587

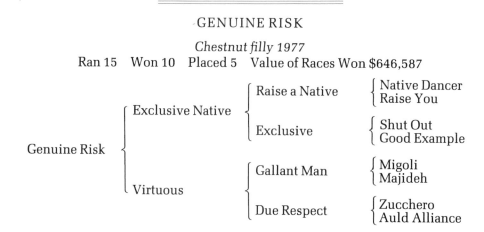

TWELVE

Emancipation and Ron Quinton

Gertie is not a name one associates with a lady. It would seem more aptly bestowed on a kitchen maid. But have no reservations, for the Australian filly Emancipation who gloried in this nickname was an aristocrat of the most blue-blooded variety despite her tendency toward the kind of temper tantrums one might only expect to see downstairs in the servants' hall.

Like many a grey, Gertie – or Millie as her trainer Neville Begg often more generously called her – was a prima donna. When she joined Begg's stable a place in a chorus line or corps de ballet appeared likelier than the 1983–4 Australian Horse of the Year title and a niche in Australian Turf history. Emancipation was a fearsomely high kicker, leaving hoofmarks 3 metres up her white-washed stable walls. Fortunately she matured with age into a top quality race mare who won 19 of her 28 races, including 6 Group I events, for $550,510. However one should not form the impression that the capricious lady was ever completely cured and until the day she retired in June 1984 Emancipation flatly refused to co-operate when asked to perform away from her Sydney base. Of those 19 victories all bar 2 at Melbourne's Flemington were gained in Sydney at Rosehill (7), Randwick (5), Warwick Farm (3) and Canterbury (2).

It is frequently said that behind every successful man there is a supportive female. In the case of Emancipation the axiom is reversed because without the quiet, methodical skills, and above all, loyalty, of jockey Ron Quinton who partnered her to 18 of those wins, there is no telling how self-destructive her mercurial temperament might have become. Although not enjoying the international reputation of a Breasley, Hutchinson or Moore, Quinton has ridden over 1,800 winners and is one of the hardest-working riders Australia has ever produced. He says:

"I suppose I work harder at the game than a lot of other jockeys but the truth is I just love it. I like to know about the opposition, no matter what sort of race it is. I like to know where horses race in a field, their riders, their colours and their barriers. You have to keep all those things in your mind and when the barriers open you can adapt to any situation. You can't dead-set plan how a race will be run but you can be well armed about what might happen."

Quinton's splendid balance, and an ability to get the most from his mount with hands and heels only, meant he was the natural partner for a feisty mare like Emancipation. It is no coincidence that fillies feature prominently among his tally of big race wins – Affectionate in the 1970 Queensland Oaks, Analie in the 1973 AJC Oaks, Sufficient and November Rain in the 1975 and 1981 runnings respectively of the same event. Born on February 22nd, 1948, in Mendooran, west New South Wales, Quinton learnt to ride on a horse called Travel On owned by his father's employers. "Dad used to train him in the early stages and I'd hack him occasionally. The people who owned the horse then arranged for me to be with Theo Green when they knew I wanted to be a jockey." He had his first ride at 17 and won the apprentice premiership once and was runner up twice in the space of 4 years. Quinton's working relationship with Randwick trainer Neville Begg then developed and, with the stable playing an influential role, he became Sydney's champion jockey for the first of 8 occasions in 1969–70.

Quinton's undying loyalty to Begg was to comprise a vital cog in the Emancipation success story because during the 1983–4 season he was also the regular jockey of leading three-year-old colt Sir Dapper. When the inevitable confrontation between mare and colt materialized in the W. S. Cox Plate Quinton stayed loyal to his mentor's filly despite holding Sir Dapper in the highest possible esteem. Even when this initial clash was lost (both horses finished behind Strawberry Road) and Sir Dapper beat Emancipation in the Expressway Stakes Quinton still refused to desert the filly. He received his reward when Emancipation recovered to defeat Sir Dapper in their 2 subsequent meetings, Rosehill's George Ryder Stakes and Randwick's All Aged Stakes, thereby securing the coveted Racehorse of the Year award. Success in these Group I events derived in no small measure from 2 faultless tactical rides which saw Quinton steal the initiative from his arch-rival Mick Dittman, his replacement on Sir Dapper. It would not be far off the mark to suggest that the measure of Emancipation's greatness is her overall triumph in the series with Sir Dapper, a champion in his own right, and for that she must thank Quinton. Few mares in Australian Turf history have retired with greater honour than Emancipation. Old-timers spoke of the indefatigable Tranquil Star who won 22 of her 102 starts in the 1940s; in the late 50s Wenona Girl might have given Emancipation a run but the grey was in a class of her own as far as other recent females were concerned.

Emancipation and Ron Quinton

To her trainer, a man with a penchant for fillies but one who uses praise sparingly, Emancipation was quite simply, "The best I have trained and I think she ranks with the greatest of all time to have raced in this country. She is a champion. Of that there is no question."

A cursory glance at Emancipation's family tree is sufficient confirmation of a pedigree steeped in class. Her sire Bletchingly won 4 of his 5 races, most notably the Group I The Galaxy Stakes, and represented the foremost Australian sire line of Star Kingdom and when sent to the Widden Stud 200 miles north west of Sydney he proceeded to emulate his grandsire. Thanks to Emancipation and the famous gelding Kingston Town, Bletchingly's progeny had won over 400 races and $4,000,000 by the end of the 1984 season, earning him 3 consecutive sires' championships. Although the son of another brilliant racehorse in Biscay, it is the name of Bletchingly's grandsire which inevitably attracts all the attention and as Star Kingdom also appears in the fourth remove of Emancipation's distaff pedigree his contribution to the mare's success cannot be overestimated. Rated the second best English two-year-old of 1948 (to Abernant) he won 9 of his 16 races and was unquestionably the fastest performer ever imported into Australia. Once installed at the Baramul Stud he smashed almost every record in sight. He became champion sire 5 times, champion sire of two-year-olds 7 times and champion broodmare sire 3 times. His strong point was naturally speed yet his great grandson Kingston Town was only narrowly defeated in the Melbourne Cup over 2 miles. It was just such a mix of blinding speed and honest-to-goodness guts which surfaced in Emancipation.

Star Kingdom's presence on the distaff side of Emancipation's pedigree appears courtesy of another grandson Gunsynd, the sire of her dam Ammo Girl. Gunsynd was a tough grey and the undisputed mile champion of 1972 whose fighting qualities much endeared him to the public. In both looks and character there was a lot of Gunsynd in Emancipation. His grey daughter Ammo Girl, conversely, was an unknown quantity since she never ran (on account of suspect legs) and Emancipation was her first foal. She had been purchased as a yearling for $1,700 by Mr M. C. Hough of Narromine Farm in New South Wales from the noted trainer Tom Smith. As if trying to be awkward from the outset Emancipation was a very ugly yearling and when first seen by a representative of the Muskoka Farms partnership in whose name she would race on lease, his comments were far from complimentary. "A big, lanky grey filly, all legs, light in condition and with a mule-like head," is how Les Young described her. But he was impressed by the way she moved. "I spent a couple of hours in the dry paddocks and even though she didn't look much she seemed pretty athletic." The leasing deal went ahead and Gertie was sent to the Muskoka establishment at Wiseman's Ferry for 6 weeks' pretraining designed to knock off the rough edges before she joined Neville Begg. By this stage Emancipation was beginning to justify Young's optimism. "One of our riders said she would prove outstanding because of her fluid gait," said Young. But she had one bad point also which was to display her temper by lashing out with her hind legs ("She is one of the highest kickers I've ever seen," said Young), a trait which subsequently almost led to her undoing after a race at Flemington. Emancipation kicked so high in the stripping shed that she ended up straddled across a bar and Begg had to lift her back on to the ground with the help of stable attendants.

Begg did not try to hurry the development of his temperamental filly and Emancipation did not see a racecourse as a two-year-old in the 1981–2 season. It was a day after her official third birthday (all Australian horses take their birth from August 1st) that she made her debut at Randwick in the Tellers Handicap over 1,200 metres (about 6 furlongs). On a slow track Quinton brought her home by a "long head" from the favourite French

Finale. The show was on the road. By her mid-season break in November Emancipation had won a further 5 races at distances between 1 mile and 1¼ miles, although she had not yet tackled Group I company.

All that changed in the autumn when she challenged older horses under both handicap and weight-for-age conditions, winning in succession the Light Fingers Stakes, Canterbury Stakes (Group II, over 6 furlongs), the George Ryder Stakes (Group I, over 7 furlongs) and finally the Doncaster Handicap (Group I, over 1 mile). In the Ryder at Rosehill on March 19th the Quinton – Emancipation pairing tasted victory over the crack seven-year-old gelding Manikato who had led the Australian classification over this distance for the past 3 seasons and had been rated little below Kingston Town. Although a filly had not won the Doncaster since Citius in 1966 and Emancipation had to carry 1.5kg (3lb) over weight-for-age such was her following that she still started a well-backed 5/2 second favourite to lift the massive first prize of $150,000.

Quinton tucked her in mid-division until the straight was reached, where-

Emancipation winning the Chelmsford Stakes

upon he began angling for a clear run. Initially he could make no progress but 350 metres out he spotted a tiny gap and Emancipation quickly burst 4 lengths clear and, even though the Doncaster is regarded as the toughest 1-mile race in Australia, Quinton took the luxury of easing her in the closing moments. In dead ground her time of 1.35.9 was still fast. By emulating Gunsynd's victory in the Doncaster Emancipation had brought her record to 10 wins from 13 races worth $271,460.

In between setting the Sydney tracks alight on Emancipation Quinton had been forging another successful partnership with the two-year-old colt Sir Dapper which culminated in a race record for the prestigious Golden Slipper Stakes at Rosehill, regarded as the juvenile championship of Australasia. Trained by Les Bridge, the colt won 5 of his 6 races and topped the two-year-old classification. A confrontation with Emancipation sometime during 1983–4 seemed unavoidable, leaving Quinton with an agonizing decision to make.

By the time that decision had to be made in October Quinton had won another 5 races on Sir Dapper including the Group I AJC Spring Champion Stakes over an extended 1¼ miles while he and Emancipation had won 4 races together, the most important being the Group I George Main Stakes over 1 mile in which she beat (Mr) McGinty by 2¼ lengths. Two weeks later the New Zealand colt reversed the form in the ¼-mile longer Caulfield Stakes in Melbourne. Emancipation hung badly on the turn and finished a moderate fourth.

Emancipation had frequently shown her displeasure at racing away from Sydney but the lure of the W. S. Cox Plate, Australia's premier weight-for-age event (and its fifth richest at $271,000), also run in Melbourne at Moonee Valley proved irresistible. As Sir Dapper was thought unlikely to stay the 1½-mile trip of the AJC Derby he, too, had this 1¼ mile race on his agenda. Quinton's dilemma was further complicated by doubts concerning Emancipation's own ability to get this distance in the wake of her Caulfield Stakes defeat. She had not won beyond 1,750 metres (nearly 9 furlongs) but Begg was anxious to fulfil her invitation to compete in the 1½-mile Japan Cup (worth twice the Cox Plate) in November. He was confident that the mare's increasing maturity would enable her to relax and stay the distance.

The customary strong field assembled for the Cox Plate also numbered (Mr) McGinty and Strawberry Road, winner of the AJC Derby by 5 lengths in 1983 but only sixth in the Caulfield after suffering problems with a lung virus and severe throat infection. Sir Dapper and Emancipation were joint favourites at 7/2. The track rode like a gluepot and Strawberry Road, who had several victories on rain-sodden ground to his credit, won as he liked. Sir Dapper came fourth but Emancipation could beat only 2 of the 13 runners

Emancipation beating Sir Dapper in the George Ryder Stakes

in what was the worst performance of her life.

Both Sir Dapper and Emancipation took holidays prior to the Sydney autumn carnival and the remainder of the 1983–4 season is really the story of their head-to-head battles and the intense rivalry it engendered throughout the entire continent. Sir Dapper drew first blood in the 6-furlong Expressway Stakes, leaving the mare on the Randwick turn to win by 2 lengths. Before the rematch could take place Emancipation had racked up 3 straight wins. She took revenge on Strawberry Road in the Apollo Stakes over 7 furlongs and just managed to fight off Trissaro in the Chipping Norton Stakes by a short head. In so doing she equalled the 1-mile track record and ran the last 800 metres in 46.7 seconds, some 3 seconds faster than the first, a phenomenal finishing drive. Then she put up a magnificent display to crush a tip-top collection of fillies in the Grade I Rosemount Wines Classic over $7\frac{1}{2}$ furlongs on March 31st. In her only foray into handicap company all season Emancipation carried a record weight of 60kg and conceded up to 8kg to her 15 opponents. Next time out the runner-up won a listed race and the third was pipped at the post in the Doncaster Handicap. Although Sir Dapper had won twice there was never any possibility of Quinton switching partners for the George Ryder on April 7th. The public were beginning to call her "Gertrude Town" after the awesome black gelding, such was her burgeoning reputation.

Rosehill was packed to capacity for this $100,000 Group I event which Emancipation was attempting to win for the second time. Bookmakers slightly favoured the colt at 5/4 with the mare at 6/4. The other 6 runners scarcely mattered.

Quinton shot Emancipation into an immediate lead, a move made doubly significant by virtue of Sir Dapper slipping at the start and thereafter being unable to extricate himself from a pocket on the fence. As soon as Quinton realized his rival's predicament he kicked on and had stolen a 2-length advantage with 200 metres left to race. Quinton's quick-thinking manoeuvre proved incalculable for once clear of trouble Sir Dapper ate up the ground to be only a half-neck in arrears at the line.

The public clamoured for a decider but the colt was scheduled to visit Queensland for the Brisbane winter carnival and there was even talk he had run his last race. However his connections found it impossible to turn a deaf ear to the unprecedented request from the AJC Committee that they run him just once more, "for the sake of racing", against Emancipation in the All-Aged Stakes (Group I) at Randwick at the end of April.

All Australia, it seemed, watched this epic encounter. Sir Dapper's misfortunes in the Ryder convinced most punters he would prevail over this longer trip and they backed him down to 13/8 on favourite. They disregarded the fact that he was bred to sprint, that Randwick's mile was considered the stiffest in the country and that he had not won over it. The mare's supporters happily recalled her scintillating victory in the Doncaster over this course and distance and eagerly accepted the 7/4 odds laid against her.

After another heart-stirring contest it was Emancipation's disciples who were able to crow. Quinton again elected to set the pace but although Sir Dapper reached the mare's flanks entering the straight, and may even have got his nose in front momentarily, his effort faltered and Australia's favourite female drove on for a decisive ¾-length victory.

However, as in so many instances of alleged "deciders", the loser returned with valid excuses. Sir Dapper had incurred a bad cut on the back of his near-fore, sufficiently deep in fact to induce his immediate and definite retirement, which might explain why he hung under pressure in the last few yards. In her defence Emancipation ran the last uphill 800-metre stretch in 45.8 seconds, another exceptional piece of sustained galloping. Who is to say that her great heart would not have responded and Sir Dapper dared to pass.

The end had come for Sir Dapper and in retrospect the curtain should also have descended on Emancipation's career. Instead she travelled north for the Brisbane festival at Doomben and Eagle Farm in May and June where she failed to win any of her 3 races. The combination of the alien environments she hated and the 59½kg she was asked to carry on each occasion undoubtedly contributed to a disappointing encore.

In a matter of 2 months Quinton had seen both his prize mounts retired. He bore the twin blows stoically, though he was adamant the mare would have been even better as a five-year-old. The Muskoka Farms syndicate agreed but the lease agreement had now expired and owner-breeder Mark Hough wanted her to commence a stud career. Accordingly the Stefan Sprint at Doomben on June 23rd was the last of her 28 races and she was sent to New Zealand to be mated with Vice Regal. Her first foal, a colt, proved one of the most sought after lots at the 1986 sales.

The durability of antipodean racehorses is renowned and Emancipation was no exception to the rule. Few European fillies would cope with a four-year-old campaign involving 15 races spread over 11 months, let alone win 9 of them including 4 of Group I status. Yet Emancipation, aided by the cultured skills of Ron Quinton, did just that.

EMANCIPATION

Grey filly 1979
Ran 28   Won 19   Placed 1   Value of Races Won $550,510

Emancipation	Bletchingly	Biscay	Star Kingdom / Magic Symbol
		Coogee	Relic / Last Judgement
	Ammo Girl	Gunsynd	Sunset Hue / Woodie Wonder
		Miss Wendy	Sostenuto / Victory Piper

THIRTEEN

Oh So Sharp and Steve Cauthen

One day in the late 1970s, so the story goes, a visitor to Walton, Kentucky, searching for the home of Steve Cauthen was advised, "Drive 70 miles up the Interstate Highway and look at the sky – there's a star in the east."

The emergence of this jockey prodigy was indeed looked upon as nothing short of divine intervention. "The Kid", as he was dubbed, was a natural. At the age of 7 he astonished one Kentucky trainer by pacifying the most volatile resident of his barn and from the age of 11 he had dedicated himself to becoming a jockey. He rode his first winner aged 16 at River Downs on May 17th 1976. The very next year he won 487 races worth over $6,000,000, won 3 of the prestigious Eclipse Awards and was voted Sportsman of the Year by *Associated Press*, *Sporting News* and *Sports Illustrated*. In 1978 he partnered Affirmed to the American Triple Crown. It seemed Cauthen could do no wrong. Both trainers and horseplayers sang his praises. "Steve Cauthen is no 18-year-old," joked Affirmed's trainer Laz Barrera, "he's an old man! Sometimes he makes me believe in reincarnation. Maybe he had another life where he was a leading rider for 50 years. That's how much he knows about his business." Others concurred. "The kid is 16 going on 35," said one. "Natural ability is one thing but I've never seen such a case of natural knowledge."

Cauthen's god-given genius had been perfected so exquisitely that its divine origin was taken for granted. Years of riding finishes on straw bales in his father's barn and sitting in the clockers' stand at the track, for example, gave him balance, dexterity with the whip and a superb sense of pace. His ability to extract 101 percent from any animal prompted one New York gambler to deliver perhaps the ultimate citation: "When you're betting against him, the kid is poison. Pure poison."

To be champion jockey and ride a Triple Crown winner would be the high-water mark of most jockeys' lives. To do so at 18 years of age made the feat remarkable. Yet Cauthen would achieve both these feats a second

Oh So Sharp and Steve Cauthen

time on the other side of the Atlantic, something no jockey had ever achieved. On this second occasion the horse in question was a beautifully bred, sweet-tempered chestnut filly called Oh So Sharp. While some critics might belittle the status of the English Triple Crown for fillies in comparison to that of the colts it has only been won by 8 fillies prior to Oh So Sharp (whereas 15 colts have been successful), and during the increasingly specialised and competitive period since the war, by just Meld in 1955. Oh So Sharp may not have been the best three-year-old of her generation but her partnership with the erstwhile "Kentucky Kid" which secured this elusive garland made the 1985 season a memorable one.

The pair richly deserved their place in the annals of the English Turf for in their own way, both overcame adversity. For her part Oh So Sharp lost 2 races in a row before the St Leger and, as her trainer Henry Cecil knew, was beginning to lose her edge after a 6-month campaign. Cauthen's fortunes had plummetted dramatically after his triumphs with Affirmed in 1978. The midas touch allegedly disappeared. He lost the ride on Affirmed during the winter of 1978–9 and experienced a much-publicised string of 110 consecutive losers at Santa Anita. "At the time a lot of people assumed I was running away from a bad losing streak but even before that I had been thinking of moving to Britain. I was getting the feeling that American racing was a day-in-day-out affair, 365 days a year and as there was no let-up it was easy to get stale very quickly."

Consequently, Cauthen duly arrived in March 1979 at Barry Hills' Lambourn yard with a retainer to ride for Robert Sangster. Within weeks Cauthen gave notice that the magic touch had not deserted him. He won on his first ride (Marquee Universal at Salisbury) and landed the 2,000 Guineas aboard Tap on Wood. Ironically the horse they beat was Kris, eventually to become the sire of Oh So Sharp. That first season, always liable to be a sighter and not the sensation imagined by the popular press, saw Cauthen notch 52 winners, a figure which rose with increasing experience of the English game to 61, 87, 107, 102 and, finally in 1984, to a total of 130 which made him only the third American jockey after Lester Reiff (1900) and Danny Maher (1908 and 1913) to win the jockeys' title. Reiff and Maher also succeeded in the classics, as did other Americans Tod Sloan, "Skeets" Martin, Matt McGee, Frank O'Neill and Lester's brother John. None of them, however, won a Triple Crown or established such a rapport with a filly as Cauthen did with Oh So Sharp.

Matching Lester Piggott's achievement of riding a Triple Crown winner must have been particularly satisfying because it was he whom Cauthen replaced as Henry Cecil's stable jockey. The contrast in riding styles was pronounced. Piggott, bottom high in the air when waiting to pounce and controlled venom when at daggers-drawn; Cauthen, low in the saddle, practically a second skin to the horse beneath, only the pumping elbows toward the finish disturbing his motionless crouch. "You could serve drinks on the kid's back at the furlong marker and you wouldn't spill a drop before he hits the wire," is how one Belmont regular put it. Obviously Cauthen recognised the need to adapt his style to the diverse tracks and tactics of English racing.

"In America the horses jump off and go almost flat out from the start. They finish slower whereas in England they often run the last quarter faster than any other. Dirt is more regular and you don't get such drastic changes in the ground. But the most fundamental adjustment is learning to balance horses over undulating courses. In America as the tracks are flat the jockey has to sit up the horse's neck and balance himself so as not to slow its movement down. I had to learn to shift my weight wherever the horse was going uphill or downhill.

In the spring of 1985 no ride was more keenly anticipated by Cauthen than that on Oh So Sharp, unbeaten in her 3 juvenile races at Nottingham, Sandown and Ascot. In the Solario Stakes she dispatched the 2 colts Young Runaway and St Hilarion with an impressive piece of acceleration up the Sandown hill and later in September she reproduced that quality to defeat the smart Deauville winner Helen Street in Ascot's Hoover Fillies Mile, a 1-mile event which since its inception in 1973 had served as a reliable guide to the following season's classics. Quick As Lightning won in 1979 before taking the 1,000 Guineas while placed horses Gaily (Irish 1,000 Guineas), Dunfermline (Oaks and St Leger) and Circus Plume (Oaks) likewise realised their potential. Helen Street continued the record of the latter by winning the Irish Oaks, a magnificent effort yet one paling beside the achievements of Oh So Sharp.

On breeding Oh So Sharp could not be sure of staying the Oaks distance and certainly not the extended 1¾ miles of the St Leger. She was from the first crop of Kris who despite that defeat by Tap on Wood, was the champion miler of his generation and in fact lost only once more (to the 1980 2,000 Guineas winner Known Fact) during a 16-race career which encompassed victories in the St James's Palace, Sussex and Queen Elizabeth II Stakes. Stronger expectations of stamina lay in the bottom line of Oh So Sharp's pedigree. Her dam Oh So Fair won over 1¼ miles in Ireland before producing 14 foals in her first 15 years at stud, 7 of them winners. My Fair Niece was placed in the Ribblesdale and Galtres Stakes, both 1½-mile races, while Roussalka won the 1¼-mile Nassau Stakes at Goodwood two years running when trained by Henry Cecil.

The new teaming started brightly when they won the Nell Gwyn Stakes over 7 furlongs of Newmarket's Rowley Mile a fortnight before the Guineas because 4 of the previous 9 winners had used this race as a stepping stone to victory in the classic, including Pebbles a year earlier. Nevertheless the 1985 1,000 Guineas took some winning. A further 6 of the top 16 females in the European Free Handicap faced Oh So Sharp on May 2nd – Triptych, Aviance, Antarctica, Al Bahathri, Bella Colora (second in the Nell Gwyn) and Dafayna – in addition to Vilikaia who had just beaten Antarctica in the Prix Imprudence at Maisons-Laffitte. With conditions good-to-firm underfoot and a brisk tailwind blowing, the competitiveness of the race would be endorsed by a time of 1 minute 36.85 seconds (half a second faster than the 2,000 Guineas), the fastest recorded in either of the Newmarket

Oh So Sharp winning the Nell Gwyn Stakes

classics since the introduction of electronic timing in the 1950s and the fastest 1,000 Guineas of all time.

As the runners descended into the dip, backers of the 2/1 favourite looked exceedingly downcast. The leaders, Bella Colora and Al Bahathri, gave no indication of stopping and Oh So Sharp had some 3 lengths or more to make up. The filly's initial reaction to Cauthen's whip reclaimed half the deficit but the principal danger to the 2 leaders seemed to be materialising from the white-faced Vilikia on the extreme outside of the quartet. Then, in one electrifying moment as the rising ground was met inside the final 100 yards, Oh So Sharp began an unstoppable surge that saw her inexorably close the gap. Vilikia's effort died and though the 2 on the rails gave every ounce and were certainly not surrendering, Cauthen had roused Oh So Sharp in the nick of time. The trio flashed past the post in unison and some minutes elapsed before the judge gave the verdict to Oh So Sharp by a short head from Al Bahathri with Bella Colora a similar distance behind.

Oh So Sharp's stock rose when Al Bahathri won the Irish 1,000 Guineas and Triptych beat the colts in the Irish 2,000, and the manner in which she flew up the Newmarket hill dispelled most peoples' reservations concerning her ability to last Epsom's $1\frac{1}{2}$ miles. Indeed, such was her progress on the gallops that Cecil left her amongst the Derby acceptors until the last possible moment in case any accident befell Slip Anchor.

"I knew from riding out Slip Anchor that the colt was absolutely right but as I was not riding Oh So Sharp in her work all the time I had to accept what other people told me about her. Henry said that she would certainly stay the $1\frac{1}{4}$ miles and win the Oaks and events proved his point emphatically."

After Slip Anchor's 7-length victory in the Derby Oh So Sharp was a 6/4 favourite to complete an Epsom classic double for trainer and jockey. In very soft ground Cauthen wisely stayed close to the early leader Romantic Feeling and tracked Triptych over to the better ground under the stands rail when the Irish filly took the lead in the straight. Thereafter all doubts about the result vanished as Oh So Sharp sprinted away from Triptych to cross the line a majestic 6 lengths in front. The terribly slow time induced by the ground failed to disguise the excellence of Oh So Sharp's performance to the extent that defeat in her future programme of Goodwood's Nassau Stakes, the Benson & Hedges at York and the Champion Stakes could not be envisaged.

It was therefore never intended that Oh So Sharp should compete in either the King George or the St Leger for these had been earmarked for Slip Anchor. However, an injury to his near-fore revised the filly's schedule and she substituted for him in both instances.

Although 5 fillies had won the Ascot race only Pawneese in 1976 came direct from victory in the Epsom Oaks. Oh So Sharp was made a 5/4-on favourite to become the second. Confronting her were the Irish Derby winner and Epsom Derby second Law Society, Rainbow Quest, winner of the Coronation Cup (and later the Arc) and the ex-Australian horse Strawberry Road, once a fierce rival of another champion filly in Emancipation, and recently the winner of the Grand Prix de Saint-Cloud. Also in the field was the Dick Hern-trained three-year-old Petoski, nowhere in the Derby but a good winner since of the Princess of Wales's Stakes at Newmarket.

The going at Ascot turned out exactly opposite to that which prevailed on Oaks day and the King George runners led by Rainbow Quest's pacemaker August rattled through the first mile in 1 minute 36.08 seconds placing

Grundy's race record of 1975 very much under threat. Inevitably the early gallop told and as Oh So Sharp began her challenge she had to swerve in order to avoid the tiring Infantry. Notwithstanding this interference she stuck her pretty head in front at the furlong pole only to be worn down near the finish by Petoski who escaped from behind a wall of horses to charge up the centre of the track and beat her by a neck. "Had he been closer to us my filly would have had time to hit back," Cauthen explained. "As it was she never even saw him. She is a great filly who ran a great race and I am making no excuses."

Oh So Sharp fulfilled her York engagement and once more started an odds-on favourite but in a race notorious for its inexplicable results she provided another name to set beside the likes of Brigadier Gerard and Grundy after Lester Piggott had steered the 1984 St Leger winner Commanche Run to a surprise $\frac{3}{4}$-length victory. In a tactical battle from the outset Piggott successfully dictated the pace, gradually increasing the gallop into a 46.87-second last $\frac{1}{2}$ mile. "I was sitting on Lester's tail and felt that he was playing into my hands by setting such a steady pace," Cauthen told the press, "but when Commanche Run quickened my filly could not go with him and I never felt I was going to win. It has been a long season for Oh So Sharp and she has been on the go since the spring."

Cauthen's final comment seemed particularly ominous in the wake of Slip Anchor's disappointing reappearance at Kempton on September 6th for his defeat meant that Oh So Sharp would stand in for him at Doncaster eight days later. Albeit by default, Oh So Sharp was afforded the opportunity of achieving the fillies' Triple Crown.

Whether winning the English Triple Crown is a more arduous task than accomplishing its transatlantic counterpart is highly debatable. The English involves 3 races ranging in distance from 1 mile to $1\frac{3}{4}$ miles, 3 totally contrasting types of track and covers 4 months of the season whereas the American version comprises 3 races between $1\frac{3}{16}$ and $1\frac{1}{2}$ miles compressed within the space of 5 weeks, on virtually the same type of dirt track. Both require durability of a sort, the former to overcome the longer time factor and the latter to endure 3 strenuous contests in one brief period of intensive competition. However, Affirmed needed to remain at his peak for about a month; Oh So Sharp had to scale 3 individual summits and on this last occasion move up to a distance of $1\frac{3}{4}$ miles less than 4 weeks after being specifically prepared for a Group I race of $1\frac{1}{4}$ miles. Henry Cecil believed his filly could do it but acknowledged the difficulties. "Another week and it might have been too late. She was beginning to go and I was just hanging on to her."

If Oh So Sharp stayed the trip little likelihood existed of her being beaten. An injury to Petoski meant only 2 Derby colts stood their ground and one of those was her stable companion Lanfranco (fifth at Epsom) to be ridden by Lester Piggott in his final English classic. Consequently the field of 6 was the smallest at Doncaster since Pretty Polly also frightened off all bar 5 in 1904.

Piggott's sole chance of retiring with a 30th classic victory lay in forcing the pace in the hope of exposing any flaws in the filly's stamina. He attempted to dictate affairs as he had on Commanche Run but in contrast to York Cauthen this time knew all there was to know about the capabilities of his major rival and kept Lanfranco well within range. Indeed the surprise of the race was just how early Cauthen chose to take up the running. "It is not a good thing being tied down to a set of instructions because once the starting gates open it all changes," he says. "As long as I know the main thing about the horse I'm riding I can react to the way the race goes and still get the best out of the horse in question."

In their sixth race together the American judged it prudent to strike

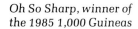

Oh So Sharp, winner of the 1985 1,000 Guineas

with his filly once Lanfranco's gallop began to drop at the 3-furlong marker. With the wind in their faces and Lanfranco and Phardante nipping at their heels, Oh So Sharp and Cauthen battled up that long Doncaster straight into the history books. Never benefiting from more than a length's advantage throughout an agonisingly protracted last $\frac{1}{4}$ mile (Cauthen reckoned she idled in front), the gallant filly possessed sufficient reserves to hang on by $\frac{3}{4}$ length despite drifting off a true line and prompting a stewards' inquiry. Fortunately within a few minutes justice was done and Oh So Sharp's victory confirmed.

For everyone concerned with Oh So Sharp the season could not have concluded more satisfactorily. Horse, jockey, trainer and owner (Sheikh Mohammed) headed their respective tables. Cauthen and Cecil had won 4 classics, only the seventh and sixth to do so in 171 years.

The filly's seasonal earnings came to £311,576 yet in truth she had won much more than this. Commercial interests may appear to embrace every aspect of modern flat-racing but no amount of money could buy the affection which Oh So Sharp and Steve Cauthen won from the English racing public thanks to their sterling exploits at Newmarket, Epsom and Doncaster.

OH SO SHARP

Chestnut filly 1982
Ran 9   Won 7   Placed 2   Value of Races Won £355,918

Oh So Sharp	Kris	Sharpen Up	Atan
			Rocchetta
		Doubly Sure	Reliance II
			Soft Angels
	Oh So Fair	Graustark	Ribot
			Flower Bowl
		Chandelle	Swaps
			Malindi